About the Author

I was born into a large family. There were ten children altogether. I had one older brother and two older sisters along with two younger sisters and a twin brother. Thus, with the seven surviving children, there were also, unfortunately, three children who didn't survive their infancy.

The children in order were Barry, (triplets) [Christine, Mary dec., Lois dec.,] Maureen, (twins) [Grant and Steven], Brenda dec, Josephine and Karen.

That's right, triplets and twins in the family.

I had a normal country upbringing. We were taught to address others, particularly adults, as Mr or Mrs and respect expected at all times. Dad was the only breadwinner and as Mum never drove a car she was happy to maintain the home.

I started work with the Tasmanian Government Railways (T.G.R) at Dunorlan in June 1973. I progressed through the rail operational grades and then transfered over into the locomotive grades to become a driver.

I retired on 30th July 2021. However I retained a casual role as a way to ease into retirement.

I live close to the picturesque town of Penguin on Tasmania's North West Coast with my wife Trudy. My two daughters are fabulous young women and are making their own way in the world.

We live on a beautiful 34 acre property with expansive views. Limousin cattle graze on lush green fields and it really is the best place to live.

I had 48 years on and around trains.

It was a hell of a ride.

Copyright © Grant Youd 2022

ISBN: 9780646871752

All rights reserved. Without limiting the rights under copyright above, no part of this publication may be reproduced, stored in or introduced into a retrieval system or transmitted in any form or by any means (electronic, mechanical, photocopying, recording or otherwise), without the prior written permission of the author.

Published by:
Grant Youd
30 Blue Wren Lane
West Ulverstone 7315
Tasmania
Australia

A Train Driver's Story

"It's been a hell of a ride"

by

Grant Youd

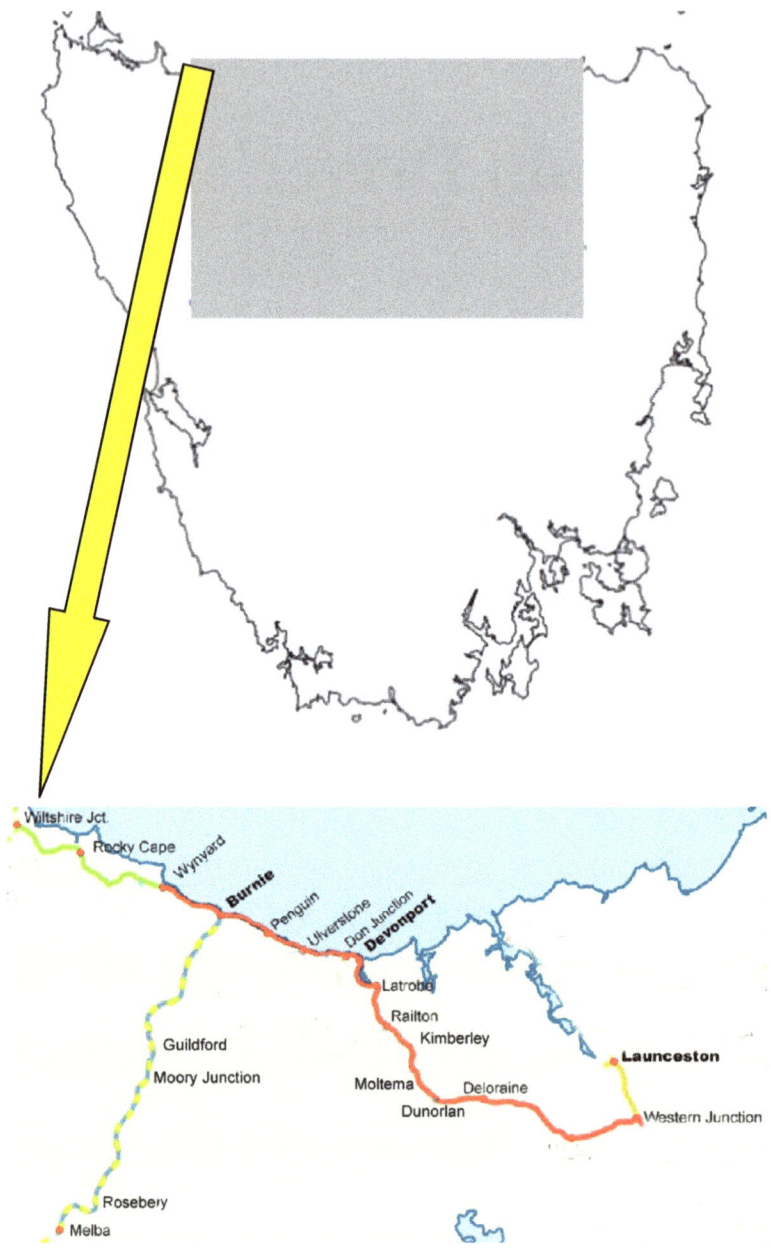

Rail lines and places mentioned in the text

DEDICATION

This book is dedicated to two outstanding gentlemen whose lives and careers were cut far too short as a result of an accident on 16th January 1986.

Harvey John Smith

Harvey John Smith and Donald Charles Atkinson are both remembered as a train crew that gave their utmost at work to helping others. Diligence and unquestioned effort was a hallmark of both men. They were good family men and admired by all.

I recall purchasing some of Harvey's beloved white canaries and several days later having to inform him that they fell off their perches. He was disappointed with that outcome but gracious as always.

Donald will be well remembered for the donning of his signature denim-like engineer's peak cap, worn proudly every day and positioned centimetre perfect on his head. His arm always rested on the locomotive windowsill with his body arched slightly outwards so as not to miss a shunter's hand signals. Dedicated to doing a good job.

Donald Charles Atkinson

They crewed together as a pair and often had a shift that saw them travel from Devonport up to my depot at Railton. We would be very pleased when they alighted the car, knowing the day's work would be done and dusted in an easy obliging manner. I remember distinctly their compatibility as workmates. There was never an ill word ever heard between them.

One ill-fated shift saw them collide with a truck near Burnie. The train was derailed and subsequently went into the Emu River.

They never made it back home to their families from work that day. It's a lesson in death to us all to understand that every day is to be cherished. It is not a given that it will be followed by another day.

Acknowledgements

To my wife Trudy, for enduring my relentless mutterings about the hassle of technology and how to navigate the process of writing my book. I would whine that, "All I want to do is write a book, not become an astronaut!!" Trudy would quite rightfully just sigh and leave the room.
      Thank You.

My sincerest thanks to all the people that I conversed with and interviewed in order to tidy up the recollections of my career.

    Barrie King
    Kevin Norris
    Phillip Moore
    Shane Malone
    Helen Holland
    Kyle Stennings
    The Don River Railway
    "Fellowship of Australian Writers - North West", in particular, their President, Allan Jamieson.

To the many people who are mentioned in this book and the other characters too many to mention. Thank you for being part of my railway journey.

Contents

Chapter	Title	Page
	DEDICATION	i
	Acknowledgements	iii
One	A terrifying time	1
Two	Early days	5
Three	Federation house fun	8
Four	The railway influence	10
Five	Lad porter beginnings	15
Six	Deloraine	19
Seven	The porter's role	21
Eight	Railton bound	26
Nine	Birds of a feather	31
Ten	Barrie King	33
Eleven	Railton lads	38
Twelve	The shunting begins	43
Thirteen	The artist at work – Ian Jordan	54
Fourteen	Things in the night	60
Fifteen	Change coming	63
Sixteen	Kevin Norris	68
Seventeen	Pranks to die for	74
Eighteen	Latrobe	79
Nineteen	Phillip Moore	82
Twenty	Ferrets working on the railway	87
Twenty One	Switch-it	93
Twenty Two	Crewing and the ressurection	97
Twenty Three	Moving towards train driving	103
Twenty Four	Finally driving	107
Twenty Five	Shane Malone	112
Twenty Six	Russell Holland	118
Twenty Seven	Train driving in scenic splendour	126
Twenty Eight	The joy of it all	137
Twenty Nine	Kyle Stennings	143
Thirty	Looking back	152

Chapter One: A terrifying time

Death came dancing at my door. I didn't know it yet but it was there outside the door, clamouring around my locomotive front steps and beating it's furious fists upon all the cab windows at once. The serenity and loneliness of the middle of the night was shattered by a sudden and frightening visitor that was hell bent on presenting me with an undeniable choice. In the next 30 seconds I would either be alive or dead and I had the unique opportunity to watch it unfold to the very end from my train's locomotive front window.

He came unannounced, with no regard or care for the forest sleeping peacefully with the night critters foraging and me just humming along minding my own business.

It was around the area of the Renison Bell Tin Mine on Tasmania's West Coast and it was about 10pm at night. I had driven the train already for four and a half hours down from Burnie to Melba Flats, approx. 130 km south. I had dropped off the empty wagons, picked up the already loaded wagons waiting there and was about half an hour into the return trip.

I was getting a tad weary. It's not easy looking at just two ribbons of steel in the searching headlights with the sustained concentration level over such a long period of time. My lulling mood was interrupted as all hell broke loose underneath my seat. I had just entered a sharp cutting and the obligatory curves therein, when a screeching noise and shaking of the loco occurred.

With no real previous experience to draw on, I forgot the unwritten rule of "If it goes really bad, you hit the brakes and hit the floor". I stood up with my hands firmly planted on top of my gauges dashboard and had feet apart as I searched for balance and the reason for it all. In a split second I had gone from massaging the train around some tight curves to a fear of imminent injury or death. I remained standing which was damn difficult when the locomotive was trying to throw me out the side window. I was in serious trouble and I just hung on. There was no time for anything. The onset of fear was the fastest thing happening by far in that cab.

The locomotives were bucking wildly under and behind me with the 1500 tonnes of copper ore beginning to argue the toss as well. My lead locomotive lurched from side to side in the cutting, the sheer rock faces straightening it up and sending it to the opposite side. Due to there only being limited clearance it actually kept the locomotives and presumably the wagons in a roughly upright position whilst crashing through it. I had eyes as big as dinner plates. It funnelled the derailed train while the track rails and sleepers were being bent and twisted like plasticine in a child's hand. The ballast flew everywhere and sleepers gouged in all directions.

The Renison mine had a water main running adjacent to the track. Its pipes were in about six metre lengths of about twenty centimetre diameter. The water pipe crossed up and over the track via a steel girder frame of substantial size. The pipe supplied the water to the mine and had a fierce pressure inside. Once on the other side of the track it was then framed back down to the ground and then again run trackside. As I was going through the cutting I invariably gathered all of the overhead steel framework with me. The crashing girder system and the sudden cannon of water pressure only added to the maelstrom. Steel girders and water pipes were flying everywhere in the headlights.

A lot went on in a few seconds and I was still at this time on my feet. My speed was slowing and the train weight pushing me was easing too. Once the cutting opened up the rock wall support was lost and the locomotives went into a seemingly slow motion sideways roll with the burying in the dirt a little more forgiving than the rock wall. The water pressure I recall bent over the young tea tree branches lining the track. It was bedlam. The locomotives rolled over slightly onto their sides and the noise and fear of death was over. The side windows had become the new floor. All the windows were intact thankfully as any breach would have been dangerous. With the steel flying around, some in the cab would have been unwanted company.

I lay there and ran a mental check on myself. Yes, I was alive and there were no injuries. I remember the flood of relief.

The complaining train and track had gone quiet and relative peace returned to the bush. I cannot remember if the locomotives were still running or not. What I do remember was the amount of effort required to get the cab door open.

My death defying crash at Renison Bell
(Photo courtesy of Wiki Ian)

Getting out was like trying to push up a manhole cover with someone standing on it. I came to appreciate the job that door hinges do in a normal circumstance. I climbed down over the side frames and wheel sets to reach the ground and then, and only then did I start to shake. It was all I could do to stand up on my trembling jelly legs. The adrenaline had done it's job. The feeling of solid ground under my feet, I recall, was overwhelming. A sense of joy and relief flooded over me and I felt almost tearful. Once I had walked a few paces my nerves calmed and normal thinking processes returned.

I was fortunate to have just enough phone reception to get a call out to train control. Most of the West Coast train line has little coverage, but it worked. After enquiring about my welfare the train controller set about organising the relief to get me home and began advising relevant people.

These days, after such events there is a very big effort put into debriefing of those involved. I certainly hoped it was my last derailment. It was very scary. I said to my relieving driver, Mr Gregory Bowen; "That was a hell of a ride. People pay good money for a ride like that at the Devonport Show."

My employer Tasrail, afforded me every assistance in regard to recuperation and with counselling to manage the emotions and reflections of it all. A couple of days off, sitting around drinking coffee and generally going easy, had me pondering how in hell did I come to be in that place a few nights earlier? I strained my memory back to preceding years and realised it was probably all my fault!!

I could go back to when I first applied to be a train driver. Or possibly it was because of my hanging over the back paling fence to watch trains go past as a longing nine year old. Or maybe it was my Mum and Dad's fault for bringing me into the world of a railway family? Perhaps it was caused by the waving train drivers that went by as I ferreted the trackside burrows for rabbits as a kid. I came to the conclusion that the latter was at fault. Of course that's where it started!!

Chapter Two: Early days

As a kid growing up around Deloraine I used to often chase rabbits, among other things that country kids usually did. Rabbiting, and in particular ferreting was something I did anytime I could.

With Butch, my terrier, and ferrets I would walk all over the countryside from Deloraine to Mole Creek and down to Kimberley. It was a rough geographical triangle – the home of rabbits. I pestered people to drive me and come back to pick me up later or went locally around on my pushbike from where we lived at Red Hills and Dunorlan, or on foot. Rabbits were on every square metre of that country. I could easily walk over all those properties covering tens of kilometres in the dark or by only partial starlight. I knew every rabbit burrow and stone heap, and the rabbits knew me too. If Butch and I walked across a paddock, I'm sure they hot footed it faster than normal with feet thudding the ground in warning.

Sometimes I took days off school. My teachers would write "gone ferreting" on the class attendance sheet and were the appreciative recipients of dressed rabbits the following day for two dollars each. My entrepreneurship was in its infancy. People often say "you couldn't get away with that today".

Deloraine High School

My gear for ferreting including Butch, was a pair of doe ferrets, six wire funnel nets made by myself, and six string nets made by Shorty Smith's wife at Deloraine. Shorty was the handyman around the school. I would have a sack bag or two for the rabbits as well.

This was a huge load to carry by one skinny kid. Skin off my shoulders from the weight of the rabbits in the bag was common. Filling each bag with only a dozen full size rabbits often meant doing two trips to get them home. It depended on the hot weather or not as to how many rabbits went in the bag.

Asking farmer's permission to go ferreting

During my primary school years we lived at Red Hills, a fertile farming area near Lemana Junction.

Lemana was the junction of the main rail line and the commencement line for the spur out to Chudliegh and Mole Creek. This line opened in 1890 and closed in 1985. The line mostly carried mixed goods and timber. Timber became the dominant freight with the requirement to supply cut pulpwood to the Associated Pulp and Paper Mills Ltd (APPM) Burnie mill. When the woodchip mills on the Tamar River opened up the line saw a lift again in the freighting of whole logs.

As kids at Red Hills we got up to all sorts of mischief. We climbed trees to harass ringtail possums and built forts in the neighbour's barn up the bank from our house.

Every pea harvesting season was eagerly awaited as it saw us climb what was called Barry's Little Blackwood Tree adjacent to our gravel roadway. We would ambush the pea trucks as they lumbered past. The trick was to climb onto a branch so as to align our long wooden poles to the truck's path and as it arrived we would shove the pole to dislodge the vines and cause them to fall onto the roadway. Once the truck was out of sight we would climb down and collect the spoils. With arms aching we carried the vines home. Mum always asked us to poke out our tongues for inspection and never expected to see anything less than green. Our evening meal was proportionately adjusted.

It was a risky job though as if the thrust-out pole got stuck in the vines on the truck we were at risk of being injured or flung out of the tree. Many bruises were gathered but by the next time we did it and the truck approached, all was forgotten. I have no doubt the truck drivers knew and some would yell out to us in the tree and laugh heartily in acknowledgement of our endeavor.

Picking wild blackberries for the table was another seasonal task.

Fishing and hunting were common escapes from the chores around the house. The worst chore by far for was to dig a hole and bury several days worth of contents from the outside toilet can. It stunk to high heaven and on occasions was a moving product. Much time was spent trying to get out of this chore. Another task was having to walk to the bush several hundred metres east of the house to pick up sticks and bark for the fireplace.

Chapter Three: Federation house fun

We moved to a new house at Dunorlan for most of my high school years. The house was an expansive Federation-style home. It had five bedrooms and two passageways. The passageways were wide and long and fun places to play. We would put mats upside down on the highly varnished floorboards and run and jump onto the mat and consequently slide as if on a magic carpet ride. We usually made it the full length of the passageway until crashing into the leadlight-filled door at the other end. Our bodies would lay crumpled like a collapsed venetian blind. Giggles then would echo down to the kitchen and mum would know what was happening. She would yell at us and say, "If you kids break that glass I'll tell your father when he gets home." We would invariably put the mats away.

Christmas saw the arrival of a plastic ten pin bowling set and the wide passageways were the ideal lanes. There were no gutter balls and the connection to the pins at the other end was almost guaranteed. It kept us out of mum's hair and away from the wrath of dad.

All of us kids would gather around the open fireplace that consumed huge wood. The more gnarled it was and knotty the better, it lasted much longer that way. We would stand in front of the blazing logs and rotate to the warmth and then have to relinquish it to someone else. Sometimes the giving up of the prime position was purely from the concept of sharing, but often it was ordered by our parents as the result of the complaining of being cold by other siblings.

I can hardly recall dad or mum having a turn before us kids. The fire, of course went out every night and every morning mum would shovel out the excess coals and ash. She would sweep the brickwork clean and use a red ochre mix on a cloth in her hand to have the entire fireplace fresh and bright. The kindling sticks and bark were placed awaiting the onset of cold in the late afternoon. This ritual was repeated every day for close to six months.

House at Dunorlan

Most rooms in the house had eleven feet high ceilings lined with ornate tin sheeting and a single hanging light cord. The varnished floors were trimmed by ten inch high skirting boards and the doors with a large gap under them was complemented by the obligatory sawdust-filled door dolly. Everything that could be done to maintain warmth in the house was important. The whole house it seemed was sorely reliant on the huge fireplaces in winter.

Like many single income families in the country we made do on meagre earnings and as each child grew older the opportunity to source a little extra income was welcome. We did odd jobs for neighbours like picking up the ever surfacing rocks from paddocks or helped dad in the bush cutting wood. It was a great expectation that the boys would follow dad on the railway.

Chapter Four: The Railway Influence

One really great fun thing was to wag school and travel with Dad who worked for Tasmanian Government Railways, and his workmates on the gang trolley.

The Tasmanian rail network is of 3'6" so called narrow guage construction. It wasn't always that way. Much procrastination and political posturing in the late 1800's, between various railway companies, with visions of opening up Tasmania to production and transport of the goods and minerals saw three differing gauges. The mainland states were afflicted with the same parochial needle in the very early days and still have differing gauges to this day. Go figure. The broad gauge of 5'3", the standard gauge of 4'8½" and the narrow gauge all got a run in Tasmania. Decades of discontent and parochaolism between the vested interests of each group led to many disruptions and failings, but it was eventually determined that the narrow guage afforded less cost and was best suited because of the terrain and bit by bit the connections of different shorter rail portions were standardised into this narrow gauge and unfolded out into the Tasmanian landscape.

The narrow gauge track, I soon learned, would have been better in wider gauge in terms of riding on a gang trolley. It protested at every curve whilst I grimly held on with ever-whitening knuckles, and it seemed not capable of holding the wheel flanges in place. What was amazing, was that the men perched on it's seats were laid back, layered in coats to protect from the 7am inch-thick frost, casually puffing on a rolled cigarette oblivious to the heaving and tossing about of the tiny trolley. I was always scared of crashing and it felt unsafe. No handrails or seatbelts. Their bodies lurched and heaved in complete unison to the trolley's movements. It seemed it was synchronised survival happening all around me.

Occasionally we needed to get off the track to allow a train to pass us. This was achieved by using a portable turntable that hung from the back of the work trolley. The turntable was positioned on the track and the trolley was pushed onto the turntable and then swung around to align with a short rail side track that was at ninety degrees The trolley would then be pushed onto the side track out of harm's way allowing the train to safely pass by. Sometimes they just didn't and collisions were common.

Portable phone for trackside use

Caricacture drawing done in charcoal. Gifted to dad's gang in 1966

The wires running on poles trackside were the communication lines between the gang workers and the train controllers along with communications to the stations. They always carried a portable phone apparatus to enable them to keep informed of train movements and the train whereabouts.

There was only one track. The train is a large propelling monster of steel and they can hurt big time if care was not taken.

The ganger would hook onto the overhead telegraph wires using a pole and connect it to the portable phone case. A series of short or long beeps similar to Morse Code allowed the call to be answered by the station that the coding indicated. Advice on train whereabouts and timings was either sought from the railway stations at the rear or in front of their current position.

Train Control would be contacted always at the start of a shift.

Once advice on train whereabouts was clear and time permitted the gang would hurriedly roll the gang trolley out on it's turntable frame and exit the the gang trolley shed and onto the main track. Placing the turntable frame and attaching it back on the trolley back wall was simple and quick. The portable turntable method enabled gang workers to move off the track anywhere along the section at preorganised take off points. They would stay on the track unless needing to get off to allow a train through. Occasionally though, through missed advice or rough guessing the time it takes a train to get to their vicinity, a misjudgement may occur.

Sometimes even while travelling along the track, upon rounding the bend they were confronted with an oncoming train. Things such as minor breakdowns, heavy loads, slippery tracks or simply from the difference between various drivers had changed the train's ability to move along the track in terms of speed. There were many factors.

In an imminent collision situation with a small gang trolley and a head on train approaching lives would be in danger.

I recall my Dad explaining to me about the best way to escape the gang trolley in the event of a train collision. The plan, from experience apparently was not to jump when you first see the train. Natural instincts, would, even at my young age, be telling me to get off damn quick. He assured me that it's best to stay on the trolley until the last few seconds before impact.

It seems that gang workers had learned that if you jumped early, yes, you were off the vehicle, but the danger came from the trolley and its contents of shovels, heavy crow bars, sledge hammers, picks and massive steel track jacks, along with the trolley itself. These would smash back over you with serious injury or death very likely. It was far safer to jump late and to be clear from the resultant debris shower.

I have never forgotten the reasoning, but in an imminent crash moment having the skillset to compute this and put it into effect would be very challenging. There was no cotton wool wrapped around their job.

Dad's gang and their trolley at Kimberley

For me, to wag school and load up my ferrets and gear onto Dad's trolley, and then go speeding down the train tracks between Dunorlan and Moltema and sometimes to Kimberley was huge fun. I would go ferreting until about three in the afternoon then stand trackside to be picked up by the gang at their knock off time.

That very small rail introduction grew my want to be a train driver, it eventually became true.

Chapter Five: Lad Porter Beginnings

I started on the railway in June 1973 for two weeks trial under the wing of Reg Holloway, the porter at Dunorlan, a small siding station just west of Deloraine.

My family at the time lived just up the bank from the railway station. Joseph Henry Youd, my dad, worked on the track infrastructure. His job included rail and sleeper replacements, along with any track maintenance requirements and he was known as a fettler. These fettlers usually comprised a gang of 6 men. These men had varying work ethic and were often of outward character which was to me sometimes intimidating and scary. They were the times of hard men and hard yards. A roof over their heads and food on the table I'm sure was the sole occupier of mind.

For me I guess it was written in stone to follow Dad into the railway just as my eldest brother, Barry and my twin brother, Steven, did. It was just the way. Work wasn't abundant, so to follow a predetermined path was almost inevitable. Lineage was common in a workplace then and particularly with Tasmanian Government Railways.

It was a formidable task for my Mum, Elvie Francis Youd and my father to care for over a family of 10 children.

To this day I am so grateful for the care and guidance given to all of us so as to reach adulthood with only few bumps and bruises along the way, but nonetheless well schooled in respect to others and ourselves and set on a good path.

I ponder my early memories at the railway and muse always at what went on back then. Some things were so hilarious and ridiculous that only being part of it could validate it.

My first role with Reg Holloway at Dunorlan was as a trainee lad porter. The position was at the very bottom rung in terms of climbing the ladder of train operations. Even being a lad porter felt important and of status because of the mandatory wearing of the shiny peak cap. I donned it just prior to the arrival of the morning Tasman Limited passenger train and it gave me a sense of official capacity.

My uniform with brass buttons and peak cap meant I was something special for the 10 minutes that the train occupied the line in front of our station. When the train left, the tie and cap were discarded until I donned it again for the returning afternoon Tasman Limited. It was a show.

Tasman Limited passenger train at Deloraine
(courtesy Weston Langford)

The big advantage, as in later years I realised, was working alongside a mature age man. With an odd prank or two, it groomed me for the big wide world. Working at subsequent stations with a large number of employees, I experienced a more insatiable appetite to belittle, prank and humiliate a young wet-behind-the ears beginner.

That's the thing about humans; it's one thing for them to set up and ridicule others with pranks, but to perform the prank and have smirking onlookers, well that is a whole other level. At the time with angst and gritted teeth, I accepted and absorbed their apparent pleasure and glee.

Truth be known they were educating a quick witted, defensive and outrageously extroverted lad porter to become the king of their pile in coming years. They should have known better. One Joseph Henry Youd had passed on such pranking skills to his children and they were coming.

Collection of various passenger tickets
(Courtesy of David Payne)

Although Reg Holloway was of quiet demeanour he would joke and have fun at my expense. For instance, every time a certain female passenger - whom he had an enormous dislike for (and my word she was abrasive) - pulled up in her car to make the trip to Deloraine on the Tasman Limited and return, Reg would suddenly disappear. I was left to attend her.

> She would state forcefully, *"Could I have a return ticket to Deloraine"*

No please or thank you as my parents taught. As per respect and courtesy commonly referenced by Reg I would answer with, "Certainly ma'am, so that's one ticket to Deloraine and back on our famous Tasman Limited, with her livery of red and gold?"

I was trying to be light hearted and hoping to just get it done. Sure enough she responded with venom.

> *"Well I don't see a bloody red and gold helicopter parked there do I?"*

Reg would glide by just in time to grin at me, without her seeing him smirk lest she rounded on him as well. God, where is that damn train, I thought.

Chapter Six: Deloraine

After two weeks at Dunorlan station I was seconded to Deloraine. The station master there was Mr Percy Anderson. And he was in charge. It was my first glimpse of the respect that station masters were obliged by others at work and around town. He ran the station "tight but fair."

As with any youngster that starts in any workplace there was an amount of understanding of where one fits in that needed to take place. Harsh at the time I thought, but in ensuing years it proved a necessary path to learning and one I thank Percy for. I had stepped out from the restful cocoon afforded by Reg at Dunorlan and into the maelstrom of the real world. It was full of characters that hummed of deceit, bludging, recklessness and every man for himself. It was a station with a large number of staff and seniority that was steeped in tradition. Pigeon holing of tasks was based on seniority and meant strict order of work.

I was a lad porter and it was made clear that I was only allowed to do lad porter duties. Of course I learnt that it was all relevant. I remember at Deloraine I was more of a dog's body "go fetch this and that", "here boy help with this" type of role.

The shunters that make up and break up trains along with marshalling wagons in yards were tasked with that and only that. The paper pushers, operating porters, assistant station master and station master had their roles and did only that role. It was very regimented. Where the hell was multi skilling back in those days? There was none.

My first task of the morning was to clean out the ash and coals from the open two-foot fireplace in the station master's office. Each station master's depot had a gifted supply of fire wood allocated annually depending on need. I had to have the fire burning brightly and his office warmed up prior to his starting duty at 8am. All day I tended the fire in between other jobs.

I thought I had joined the Tasmanian rail industry to play with trains, but it appeared a distantly flimsy idea. I was not allowed to play with the trains, and there was no way that I would under Percy's orders. Little did Percy know my time would come, I would get to play trains.

Deloraine Railway station
(courtesy of Howard Mulvey)

Chapter Seven: The Porter's Role

My major role was to look after the customer's goods and parcels. This was a full time job back then as the railway carted everything from matchboxes to liquor, right through to the mail and furniture.

There were not the trucks on the road as today. Small trucks and courier vans were buzzing back and forth from the railway station to Deloraine businesses. They even included deliveries to outlying towns such as Meander and Exton. It was the centre of activity and I was flat strapped keeping up.

The skill was to organise the stacking in the expansive store rooms in reverse order to their collection. It was hell to get a fridge or bedroom suite for a customer when it was buried by tonnes of goods in front of it. I had to keep out what I knew, or at least second guess, was going to be collected shortly.

Business owners were prompt because they needed their goods. Farmers were terrible at picking up their items. Apparently it was up to the weather, spuds going in or out and when the cows needing milking.

My storeroom was ordered chaos, with many tonnes of goods locked away overnight and sometimes for weeks. I grew a sense of ownership over their goods and parcels. Van loads of alcohol were piled in. You could set your watch by the mail bags to go in and out for the Post Office, but the massive piles of alcohol in cartons were dribbled out because it was adjusted to sales and customer demand at the pubs and clubs. My storeroom was used as a pseudo storage facility and it was free. It didn't help my efforts to try and create a fluid flow in and out of parcels though.

Sometimes goods like vanity units, ovens and the like spent the night under the very ornate verandahs of the Deloraine Railway Station. The police station, being a stone's throw away, was some comfort. Back then it sufficed. Fast forward to the end of my forty eight years service and the police station could have been in my storeroom and those goods would not be there the next morning. These days it seems that everything inanimate has legs.

The asphalt platform surface was a nightmare. I was required to unload products from the wagons. Machinery, fencing materials and so on would often come in open topped wagons with drop down side doors. These open wagons were ideally suited to irregular shaped and awkward loadings. Asking other staff to assist with heavy items was often met with scowls of, "Its not my job," but Percy's intervention usually sorted it.

The platform was sloped in nature to allow rain run off, but the smoothness of the surface was questionable. Uneven bits of patch ups were trip hazards while struggling with an awkward farm implement. The wheelbarrows, used for smaller goods and parcels were another thing all together.

Most goods and parcels arrived in box wagons. These were often sealed with metal seals to deter theft and weatherproofed to protect the items. About the only way to get the sack (that is, fired) was to steal a customer's produce or goods. The seals were also to deter prospective thieves trackside.

I would be required to unload tonnes of customer items and parcels out of these wagons by wheelbarrow and move down a metal ramp placed to bridge the gap between the platform and the wagon. My barrows were of different sizes and shapes that depended on the goods needing to be moved. I had a standard 2-wheeled hand trolley, and a 3-wheeled barrow with a single wheel at the front. It was a terror to take off sideways on the sloping platform and it was a strategic exercise to load it so there was at least a chance it would go in the direction that it was pushed. It often refused and ended up careering into other packages on the platform or even lurching in a freedom flight to escape to the train tracks below. Howls of laughter followed from the other staff, but only in rank up to the station master. At Percy's level it was not humorous. Percy was where the humour stopped. It stopped as suddenly as my laughing colleagues disappeared when Percy stepped out of his office to see what the ruckus was. But Percy always had my back. He had been in my shoes decades before.

My best barrow was a rectangular one sort of shaped similar to a single bed. It had 4 wheels and was suited to movement forward and backwards. It was important to load it evenly and have it loaded in line so as to move it straight ahead to the store room. It would carry an awful lot at a time, something like two or three ovens or twenty to thirty cartons of beer. The weight on it was only commensurate of my ability, at barely sixty kilograms to push it up a slope to the storeroom. Sometimes a pang of compassion would well up in someone and they would help. My customers would often help.

Typical barrows used for goods and parcels.

The pranks and their scope knew no bounds. My first recollected incident was when "Mr Nobody" greased all my barrow handles with graphite grease. It was easily accessed in any rail yard as it was used to grease switch points and throw over levers to prevent wear. It was black, messy and a bloody pain in the back side to remove. My storeroom door handles were another target. It would only occur occasionally so as to allay suspicion.

Small bag barrow

Grease in the fingers of my gloves was another mongrel trick. This one was worse as I would have to go to the station master for another pair from his secret treasure trove of chattels, but I was never able to explain the apparent careless misplacement of my issued pair. That's another thing I learned; what happened at work, stayed at work.

All the while, my brain was becoming more and more conditioned to be watchful and alert to the escalating elaboration of the pranks. Grease in the glove fingers was soon kindergarten level in stature. Some pranks would slowly and meticulously evolve and build over weeks to culminate, in the perpetrator's eyes, as the ultimate victory. It was a game and competition as the King of Clown's mantle was much sought after. I was yet a mere peasant in the realm, but over the years I would creep up the kings' ladder and dethrone those before me. It wasn't a planned thing, but it just evolved through immersion.

Chapter Eight: Railton Bound

After about three months at Deloraine I was transferred to Railton which was to become my home station for my next twenty or so years.

Above: Railton Railway Station 1900
(courtesy of Ted Lister Collection)
Below: Railton railway site today

As a teenager without a car to drive, I would jump on the freight train heading west from Western Junction to Burnie. They'd pick me up trackside at Dunorlan where our family lived and give me a lift to Railton some twenty three kilometres away. This would occur on Monday morning's 207 freight train. I would spend the working week at a single man's hut inside the Railton railway yard and be returned back by the 236 train late Friday afternoon.

It was a progression to self independence. I had to set alarms to get up for work, cook my own meals, make my own bed and clean up. The single man's quarters consisted of a double hut set up joined by a shared shower and bathroom. I shared this with another single chap named Terry Crisp. He was fastidious with cleanliness and would not swear even if you paid him too. I saw him get his upper arm caught between the buffers once and writhing in agony on the ground, he muttered through pursed lips "curses and double curses," I would have said a lot worse than that.

He was a good companion to have as a neighbour. He was so very respectful and quiet. He left the job and moved out soon after my arrival and I was then the only occupant. On Friday nights it was with glee that I headed home to Mum's cooking. I was like a hobo jumping onto a wild west train for the surging ride back to Dunorlan and home for the weekend.

After the weekend I would catch the train back down the Kimberley bank to Railton for the week. I travelled in the guard's van at the rear of the train. There was a desk on which the guard would do his paperwork. The paperwork would include details of what wagon consist he had on the train and in what order. Also details of which wagons were dropped off or added at the various stations and sidings along the way. He kept a meticulously sorted order of the GL76 forms that had details regarding the goods and parcels to be taken from the wagons at the relevant places. He would also maintain train time running sheets as he travelled through each section of track.

The van also had a small pot belly stove for the guard to cook meals or heat up a stew. The pot belly ran on chunky bits of coal. The heat they put out was incredible and very much needed in the cold misery of a Tasmanian winter at two am in the morning in a rattling draughty van. There were a number of guards that relieved the cold via a stash of longnecks and the smell of alcohol saturated the small confines of the van.

Guard's van with much revered pot belly stove

It was very easy in those circumstances to tipple a little too much without realising it. When the train pulled up at the station platform the guard would often open the door to get out and the fresh air would collide with his inebriated senses. By the time he walked twenty paces along the platform it started to seemingly move and sway under his feet and assistance would be required to get him sat down on the platform bench seat. The train would be duly shunted and when ready to depart, the guard would stagger to his feet, climb back into the van, extend his arm out the window to signal the train driver that all was clear to depart and bid farewell.

Some drivers would deliberately go too quickly for me when being dropped off so as to not lose too much time they would say, but both driver and fireman would revel in watching me attempting to plant my feet in the ballast as I exited the train. The problem was the forward momentum of my body was faster than my legs could run and would often result in a face plant trackside with my bags and gear tangled all around me. If I was able to keep my feet I would give the guard the thumbs up and he would respond with a grin. I have no doubt that anytime I stumbled the driver and fireman would be up in the cab high-fiving and laughing the next ten kilometres to Deloraine. It was always prudent to check the rosters to see who was going to crew 236 to ready myself for the fast drop off on the way home.

Singleman's Quarters at Railton

Not long after, I attained my car licence and proudly drove my shiny HD Holden Premier with lots of chrome out of

Thurlow's Car Yard at the top end of Deloraine. Dad was my guarantor and he said he and Mum had no financial ability to help, which I knew, with payments. It was my job to ensure enough of my pay was kept aside to make the monthly payments over the next three years. Schooling in life never ever ends. I never defaulted on payments or travelled in a guard's van again.

DB Guard's Van.

Chapter Nine: Birds Of A Feather

As a lad porter at a major station such as Railton the duties were much more varied. There were more staff and there was much more to do, including wrangling pigeons.

Pigeon racing was a really big deal and people from all around the state would send pigeons by rail to a station at the required distance from their home to complete practice flights back. There would be boxes holding anything from four to twenty birds, each in separate compartments.

Sometimes small remunerations would change hands for special promptness of release and accuracy. It was "money for jam," well it was supposed to be that way anyway. The boxes would come off the train and I would place them out in a row in order according to the release times indicated. That was easy but the problem came when other owners' boxes had similar or overlapping times. It was nigh on impossible to comply as accurately as that. That's where the remuneration came in handy.

All this pigeon coordination had to be fitted in amongst loading and unloading wagons. As a consequence it was often hectic and if the pigeons were not released as required I would make an adjustment notation to the owner. When the empty boxes were returned by train they could compare and adjust their bird appraisals. This was essential and saved the lives of many pigeons. I often wondered the plight of those that took an hour longer to get back to their respective lofts due to not being released on time. Without a notation on the boxes the birds would not be considered as suitable for racing and despatched to bird heaven. I wondered how many champions were put down through no fault of their own.

Also, with congested time releases the pigeons would often congregate and fly around instead of bee-lining for home. Only after wasting a lot of time would they eventually break off and depart with their natural homing instincts taking over. They are simply amazing birds.

One of my earliest recollections of my own initiated tomfoolery came after I collected an egg from one of the pigeon boxes. They often laid an egg during transit. I placed the egg carefully inside the rim of Barrie King's porter peak cap. I was thinking that when the Tasman Limited rolled in Barrie would rush into the station and slap his cap onto his head and the egg would burst and the resultant mess would be a funny sight. Well, to this day I don't know if it happened or not. I do know that later that day, Barrie waited until I went to the toilet and upon hearing me pulling on the toilet roll holder promptly let fly with a bucket of water in through the louvre window. Among my words of fright a voice said, "Don't do that again". That's how it was, nothing else was said by either party.

Station Master's uniform
(courtesy Penguin History Group)

Chapter Ten: Barrie King

I caught up with Barrie after he finished up on the rail and he reflected on the early days. He still lives in Railton. His wife Anne has passed and Barrie's health is a tad diminished. He recalled his time with the Tasmanian Government Railways (TGR).

I started in 1955 in Devonport as a messenger boy doing odd job type of work such as delivering invoices to businesses or their agents in town. I also hauled the luggage of the passengers that moved through the platform at Devonport.

It was a bee hive back then with people off trains, freight trains shunting back and forth all day and lots of staff employed to cater for such a busy hub. Passengers on the Melbourne to Devonport ferry used to disembark on the western side of the river near where the massive cement silos currently stand. These cement silos held the pure cement produced by the then named Goliath Portland Cement Company from Railton. Especially built bulk wagons hauled it on the sloping track some twenty two kilometres to Devonport. It was pumped into the silos until a bulk cement carrier ship arrived to ship it to mainland Australia markets.

The passengers from the ferry would disembark and just for a moment in time would flood the Devonport terminal and swell the numbers already there getting onto passenger trains. There were a lot fewer cars back then and getting to employment was often by train.

Each weekday the worker's train left just after 6.15am and headed off to South Burnie, forty five kilometres west, dropping off workers along the route. It was packed with APPM workers along with those employed at the Tioxide plant. The train would then travel the short distance to Burnie town proper with any remaining Burnie workers. From

Burnie some caught the train down to Tasmania's West Coast supplying employees to the mining companies there.

BBL type passenger carriage

Original Devonport signal box levers

Another worker's train travelled from Devonport to Railton to supply the employees of the Goliath Portland Cement Company. On its return trip it would bring down workers needing to get to Devonport, along with High School children to the much larger Devonport township. It was busy as hell!!

About a year later I was called up to do National Service training at Brighton, near Hobart. After completion I returned to working porter roles at various small railway stations along the coast. These included Howth, Leith, Penguin, Moltema and Heybridge. Tasks included crossing trains and post office duties as some places had incorporated post offices. Heybridge was busy because the Tioxide plant was situated there. I spent some time at the Burnie station living in the single man's quarters.

One day, while walking into town I was struck by a speeding car with my body landing thirty five metres away from the impact point. I was unconscious for ten days and busted up badly spending many months in hospital. I was destined never to get a shunting job due to the resulting physical limitations.

In 1956 I moved to Hobart as a porter, then later back to the North West Coast to the stations at Railton, Latrobe and Devonport. I worked at whatever I could. I got some goods-shed work. I drove train crews to their respective changeover points. I recall that at Devonport one day, a certain porter was clearly inebriated and had fallen over in the station doorway and lay prone there. Many minutes of, "What the hell do we do with him?" later the station master was instructed to dismiss him of his employment. Not wanting to do that, he advised his senior inspector who came and supervised the employee's transportation to a doctor to verify the drunken status. However, a duly supplied written doctor's report stated the man was suffering from "fatigue!!"

He never did any work when he was at work, but his official employment remained intact.
   Barrie King

Early Devonport railway yard
(courtesy of Weston Langford)

Signal box Devonport

Recently, we laughed at the pigeon egg incident and Barrie has remained a friend to this day. Barrie took a redundancy when it was offered and spent his retirement on his block at Railton with Anne and his beloved beagles.

Chapter Eleven: Railton Lads

Another of my duties, whilst at Railton, was at the end of each shift where I had to clean the wick in the Eastern signal lantern and then relight it. I would clean and refresh the wick and refill the lamp base with kerosene. The light would then shine towards the oncoming train traffic during the night. The back half of the semaphore arm signal housed portions of red and green glass which I had to keep clean as well. This cleaning and maintenance was done as required every couple of days or as directed if the train drivers complained that the visibility of the signal was poor.

Semaphore signal from Latrobe Station

The station master at Railton, Mr Danny Watson, like Percy at the Deloraine station, was of the old breed. He would often smile and take pleasure at the banter going on between us, but would not often involve himself in it. He was certainly a senior station master in the state insofar as the freight and management required there.

The prominent Goliath Portland Cement Company and the Blenkhorn Railton Lime Company were significant customers in revenue and work terms. Much at Railton revolved around their dominant presence in the town.

Danny was an avid sports follower particularly of Aussie Rules Football. If we had any small misdemeanours we quickly got out of trouble by talking footy.

One of the shunters was Max. He used to cause Danny a fair share of grief. Max would declare he was heading home for a cuppa as he lived across the road from the rail yard but would often be seen going out of his yard by car a few minutes later and be gone for two hours or more. This was likely in search of a bargain buy or to procure something to later sell. He would buy and sell anything. His nickname became the very lengthy Max, Marine, Motorcycles and Mobile Homes. A nickname largely derived from his penchant to be a merchant of everything.

He once bought a cheap cow from the backblocks of Lorrina. The animal had hardly seen humans during its life and was wild as an axe on the down swing. Any attempt to restrain it was to endanger life and limb. He advertised the critter as a quiet house cow ready to milk by hand.

Another time he caught about seventy wild pigeons from old barns and derelict houses around the Dunorlan area. I know this because he enlisted my help to spotlight them one night and bag them as he handed them down to me. He subsequently plucked all seventy and sold them as plump, grain fed squabs. He was a hawker of everything. Max was a funny man with little regard for authority or rules; he was one of many on the railway.

The assistant station master at Railton was Alan Foster. You could set your clock by his timing of arrival at work, home for morning tea, home for lunch and knock off time. Alan was a stickler for properness and his resolve to maintain this was legendary. Even if a train was entering the station platform Alan would still head off home for morning tea or lunch on time. He never wavered from this, train approaching or not. Alan never drove a car so walked to his railway-supplied lovely brick home in Railton just along from the station.

Even though of high standing in officer terms, Alan was more often than not helpful whenever possible. He would even push my barrows into the storeroom. He was never at fault though. It was always someone else's fault in his eyes. Occasionally he would be caught up in some mischief and his protestations of innocence could not be defended.

Once I asked him to help me pick up and carry a bedroom dressing table to the storeroom. It was a very expensive looking piece of furniture. It had flash edgings, fitted drawers and ornately shaped full sized mirror as well as a sunken centre board for water jugs. We each took hold of an end to carry it and upon lifting it up, the mirror smashed. The station had big verandahs with massive curved beams underneath and I swear before the shattered glass crashed all around us on the platform Alan said looking up at the roof, "Who put that there?" I could not believe my ears. It was funny, but I dared not laugh until out of Alan's company.

Another time he was helping me with the four-wheeled barrow with a stack of beer cartons on it. We were going fine until he tripped on the uneven asphalt and promptly let go of the barrow. I was blamed for pushing it too hard. The barrow was last seen careering over the edge of the platform with my slight frame still hanging onto it. I went down with the ship!! It was still my fault.

Alan's son, Phillip was the total opposite to his Dad; painfully casual and laid back. Phillip's nickname was Panther, for no reason to do with quickness or fleet of foot. The nickname was derived from the original Pink Panther series of movies. His immediate full blushing colour in his cheeks when discussing sex or such topics caused great amusement. Picture magazines of partly naked women flashed in front of him coloured him up nicely.

Despite this kaleidoscope of people and their habits, there was still a sense of family from all those that worked there. We actually all got on very well, but there was the occasional funny or stupid event that tested friendships. The workplace and the people had its own sense of community about it.

I remember the time I set a springer snare among some young wattles on Alan's walking track to home. It was a path that only he walked or had a need to. After many years of walking six times a day on that path he had formed a run that any wallaby would dream of. The supple young overhanging wattle tree soon became the springer and so the snare was set. All those except the station master were in the know and waited for Alan to saunter his usual free striding way up the platform. He arrived with no apparent change of gait or steam from his ears. He just walked into the office and sat at his desk to shuffle paperwork. We were at a loss so went to check the snare and sure enough it was sprung with the keeper peg ripped from the ground and laying some metres away. Success, but Alan quite correctly would never let it be known.

While still living in the single man's quarters some two years later I awoke one night to the sound of a cow bellowing forlornly. Yes, it was Moana. Moana was aptly named and known around town for her mournful noise. She was owned by the fettler gang leader, Laurie Smith. Laurie lived in the ganger's house adjacent to the level crossing on the opposite side of the road to the station. Moana annoyed everyone every night by bellowing for no apparent reason and Laurie was either oblivious to it or just didn't care. There were houses all around, the pub and the post office, all within one hundred metres.

Laurie had tied Moana to a peg just near my single man's hut so as to give her plenty of good long feed there but she bellowed just the same anyway. I'd had enough of no sleep so I got out of bed and in my pyjamas, untied her, marched her over the main road and in through Laurie's back gate. I tied her up to his Hills Hoist clothesline and with only enough rope so as not to enable her to sit down. I went back to bed and smiled at her moaning all night long. I was hoping no one saw me and called the police. Next morning Laurie was sitting on the station platform waiting for me to start work. I believed I was in for a punching. Laurie looked at me and said "it's a long road with no turns in it, my young shaver". That's all he said and left. I was very relieved as Laurie was well known to not take mischief kindly. My work mates were watching and hoping to see me get a clip under the ear.

I got away with a lot at Railton possibly because I was a teenager still learning the ropes. I was cut slack occasionally and watching Laurie striding away was one of those times. I bet he was grinning to himself too as he couldn't allow his mean and tough reputation to be lessened by some young smart alec.

Chapter Twelve: The Shunting Begins

As a porter, there was no chance to sit down for long and rest, but at least my porter job kept me mostly out of the weather and reasonably clean. For the shunters though it was much tougher. Our uniforms were made of a thick felt-like material. The trousers on hot days were near unbearable. The material just did not breathe. The vests were of a slightly lighter material, but were still hot in summer. We often only wore the vests when the Tasman Limited was near. A clean uniform, clean polished boots were nigh on impossible.

    I qualified to become a shunter and at last I got to play trains! The dust and heat from running around all shift I realised was a real complaint from the shunters.

    We worked three shifts around the clock: 4am till 12 midday, midday till 8pm and 8pm till 4am. Our main shunt loco of choice was of the "X" class. These locomotives were the first diesel electrics to service the main line. A stable of 32 were utilised and marked the transition from steam powered trains. The United Kingdom (U.K.), English Electric Company built and delivered them from 1950-1952 and were maintained in service until 1998. With 660hp and weighing 58 tonnes they were more suitable as hauling locomotives, but whenever we could get our hands on one for yard use we jumped at it.

    Trains run at all times and normally to a set schedule however that schedule was often interrupted by yard derailments that resulted in late loadings and train marshalling. Wagons in some cases couldn't be easily pulled out of the dirt and placed back on the rails in time to make a departure time. Yard derailments were mostly small with a wheel set off or maybe a couple of wagons.

    Train delays out on the mainline were a major blow to schedules as it affected all other train movements and crossings. The blockage sometimes lasted many days. If a train derailed out there then the speed and weight equalled a momentum of force that usually created extensive damage.

Train crash aftermath at East Penguin
(Courtesy of Fred Jones Collection)

Main line derailments were common and occurred for many reasons. Customer disillusionment over late services was high. Some were because of downright poor driving skills or badly loaded wagons. Sometimes it was a result of poor train makeup whereby really heavy wagons may have been interspersed with light wagons creating excessively violent bunching forces. Track deformities such as worn rails, rotten sleepers or bad corner cants are among some of the countless reasons trains come to grief. Rock falls and downed trees were also an ever-present risk. Major flooding events were also of concern due to the very large remediation and rerail works required to bring the track back to a safe traffic level.

Major flood wash-away at Blythe River bridge 1929
(courtesy of Penguin History Group)

Navigation of these issues was something I learned later when I gained a driver's ticket. But first, I learned how to shunt in the yards. I had to make up and break up trains. It was physically hard and you needed to be fit. And I was fit.

I played country football, badminton, and chased kangaroos all over the Central Plateau in Tasmania with dad. Hounds bellowing the leaves off the eucalypt trees was music to dad's ears. He often would not even take a gun but preferred to just sit on a stump and listen to his beloved foxhounds. Tiger was his favourite, he would say, " Listen to that tune!"

I always took a gun. A single barrel shotgun made by Harrington and Richardson that kicked at both ends. My shoulder was always sore and red after a day's hunting, but I never complained to dad lest he leave me at home.

There was always an unspoken competition between us as to who shot the higher number and the champion mantle silently stayed in place until the next trip. One day down River Road at Deloraine we hunted a thick scrub filled with

Rufus Wallaby. I was standing atop a stump vigilant to any approaching animals to add to my tally. The dogs had gone quiet and shortly after dad came ambling along the track leading past my stump with his gun broken across his arm just as he taught me to do for safety. He enquired as to my tally and I replied that I had seven. He answered that he had seven as well and as the dogs had gone quiet, we would head home in half hour or so. He walked a few metres away along the track and spotted a wallaby that I had previously shot but not yet gathered. He lifted his gun and blasted my dead wallaby.

I said, "What the hell----?" He turned and smiled and said, "that makes me eight now. Call the dogs we are going home". With that kind of recreation I was very fit.

Wagon handbrake setup (anti runaway device)

Along with working out and full time chasing rail wagons, I became very fit indeed. I had a six pack of abs. The walking and running for a shunter never stopped. It went on all day, hooking up wagons, unhooking wagons then kicking them down the various marshalling yard tracks then running them down in order to brake them to a stop where required.

The coal trains from Fingal on Tasmania's East Coast came in several times a week. They were usually made up of twenty six wagons and would snake out around the bend to the Goliath Portland Cement yard. Goliath owned the coal mine and we railed the coal from Cornwall to be unloaded at their plant. Each wagon was of fifty tonne capacity. The coal was dropped from bottom doors and into a pit and on to conveyor belts and taken up to the top of a pair of towers that enabled the coal to stockpile for later use.

I used the towers for fitness training. I would wind the wagon doors open by turning a hand wheel forty three and a half complete turns, which was an exercise in itself. When the bin beneath was sufficiently empty I would go another half turn on the wheel and send a flood of coal down into the bin. I would take off out of the shed, run around the back, down steps onto a mesh walkway about sixty metres long and on an angle of forty five degrees. I would sprint up it to touch the tower and jog back down. It was much harder on the legs running back down the mesh. I would then fly up the steps around the corner and back into the unloading shed. I would then wind that goddamned hand wheel another forty three and a half turns. This exercise program needed to be done before the conveyor system had emptied the bin I just filled. It usually took three to four minutes a wagon which was a leg-burning regime. I know some drivers in the locomotive would gnash their teeth watching me do this and thought me an idiot.

Coal towers at Goliath Cement. (Australia Cement)

We also had to load and unload hundreds of heavy solid timber pallets. Laying them out on flat deck wagons we would then shunt them out to Goliath Cement yard for their men to stack the bagged cement on. Watching their workers carry and stack forty kilogram bags of cement was a reality check that our job was cushy. They were sweltering from the weight and heat in the confines of the bagging shed. The cement dust covered them so much so by end of shift they were a grey ghost walking around. Cement was through their hair, in their ears and any exposed skin was of a cement colour. It was terrible. The whites of their eyes stood out like lamps on in a foggy mist.

    The loaded wagons were then hauled back into our rail yard and marshalled onto freight trains and sent on to Devonport wharf for ship loading over Bass Strait.

    The pallets certainly were not the flimsy throwaway pine ones of these days and every effort had to be made to repair any broken or fractured ones. They were often covered in cement from broken bags and when they flopped down into their place the resultant cement dust showered back over us. Our thick uniforms could hardly breathe as it was without being clogged up with cement. It was hot and dusty work. Spreading pallets was universally hated by everyone.

Cattle, pigs and sheep were carried by rail as well in specially built wagons that no animal would escape from. They were the Alcatraz of stock crates. After these wagons were taken from the train we would take them up to be unloaded at the very heavy duty stock yards for their new owners to pick up.

Cattle wagon

The Railton rail depot had a wye. The wye is a portion of track shaped like the letter Y with an added top line at the top of the letter. The wye portion of yard track enabled wagons to be effectively turned around if required. Some major depots such as Devonport had a turntable upon which they placed a wagon to turn it around. It was basically a very large lazy susan.

Sheep wagon

Incidently, the southern leg of the wye at Railton also served as the departure track for trains heading to Sheffield and Roland. The line operated from 1914 until closure in 1957.

Early train with stock wagons
(Courtesy of Helen Holland)

Turntable used for turning locomotives or wagons

All shunting back then was done via hand signals during daylight and tri-coloured lamps by night. It was important to keep a good lookout for the shunters and their signalling. I still have my own original issued tri-lamp.

My issued tri-coloured lamp for night shunting

The trains were mostly shorter then but sometimes within yards track curvatures there was a need to relay the hand signals. One shunter at the workface would signal "ease up," or whatever he needed, to another shunter on the curve and the signal then relayed on to the driver. Care needed to be taken by the shunters to allow time for this human transmission for it to happen safely. For "ease up slowly," for example, the first shunter would open and close his arms outstretched above his head. This same movement was replicated by the second shunter and so on. Upon getting the "ease up" signal the driver would apply some deft braking on the loco and wagon brakes thereby easing up softly onto the wagons down the yard at the first shunters position.

Author shunting with X6 1981 at Railton
(courtesy of Steve Bucton)

Sometimes when only one shunter was at work and faced with a curving track and thus no visibility, the shunter would operate on the fireman's side for the signalling and then the fireman would just verbally relay the instruction. With so much human input, foggy, rainy weather conditions and the like, many signalling interpretations were misread or misjudged. All too commonly derailment or dangerous incidents occurred. There were many terse words between shunters and drivers such as, " Wave ya …arms you idiot," or, " Are you blind?"

    I remember shunting one day and I just could not get a pop on the whistle in acknowledgement from the driver or fireman in the cab. My arms were aching from waving a signal to them with no apparent recognition. As the loco was only forty metres away I picked up a piece of ballast and threw it at the loco hoping to wake them up or get them to stop their talking and pay attention or whatever it was that was causing the lack of attention. Just then the driver poked his head out the window and the stone struck him flush on the cheek. I ran up to check on him loudly shouting my anger for his non-attention to realise he had a two inch laceration to the face. All sorts of threats of retribution were tossed at me. A cloth was hurriedly sought to stem the bleeding. Although my signals were not seen because of a game of cards in play at the time, I let that slide given the bloody outcome. I felt genuinely remorseful as he was one of the nicest blokes at work.

    I'm still sorry Bruce.

These sorts of things happened every day, though not every day ended in blood.

Chapter Thirteen: The Artist At Work- Ian Jordan

The station at Railton was a sturdy strong building as all rail station buildings seemed to be. It was spacious with large waiting and store rooms. Each office had expansive bench counters with highly varnished timber and solid timber desks that took four men to carry. The desks of the paper pushers were especially built for purpose. They had four small drawers about fifty millimetres deep for biros, paper clips, staples, rubbers and so on. Below these sat deeper drawers that housed the paperwork like consignment notes and accounting files. At the back of the desk were three full cupboards for filing and document storage that was only needed occasionally.

When Ian Jordan sat at his desk he was something to watch. Ian was an operating porter whose role was to collate and file documents of all kinds relating to freighting. Ian was a lovely guy. His interaction with everyone was one of assistance and kindness. Everyone got on well with Ian. He was a pillar of help and advice, especially when stuff got rocky at work and he was so funny.

His skill at shuffling papers was special. As an artist in his gallery, so Ian was at his desk. I would watch, mesmerised, whenever he pulled out of the drawer a huge stack of consignment notes of a hundred and more to begin sorting them in number and station order. He would wriggle in his seat to be perfectly balanced and prepare to show off. He knew he was great to watch, but never ever said so. The papers each had a consignment note number on the top right hand corner and each needed to be in station sequence order as well. With licked fingers the speed was amazing. It was like watching a banknote counting machine. Ian always loved watching pranks unfold, but was never a prank starter.

Once, I put a live blue tongued lizard in his paper drawer with the view of it scaring the life out of him when his fingers raced through the papers. It was a very large lizard and the joke had a heart attack written all over it. So it just had to be done.

On arriving for my shift start, about two weeks later, I walked into the office to see paper everywhere. Papers were on all the benches and spread about the floor all over the place. His desk was completely empty and the drawers taken out. The cupboard doors were swinging free from the back.

As Ian was turning the whole desk over on its side I asked, "What's happening… ?" Ian replied, "There's a bloody rotten stink here somewhere".

He started swishing phenyl liquid all over the desk and scrubbing fiercely while cursing the smell he had decided was from dead mice. They had defiled his prized desk and he was angry. Only then did I realise I had forgotten about the lizard. I burst out in laughter. My collapsing in hysterics did nothing to appease the normally placid porter. Through tears, I explained that I had placed a great big, live blue tongue in there. We completely overturned the desk and sure enough, the lizard had apparently crawled over the back end of the drawer and been squashed to death when Ian had shoved the drawer back in. I accused him of animal welfare atrocities as I helped him remove the lizard carcase and clean the desk. Ian only ever settled down again when all papers were restored to their rightful place.

Ian spent the greater portion of his time in the office and relished the chance occasionally to get out and run about in the yard.

The Railton station was different to most because it sat with tracks running either side of it.

Train authority to occupy the track outside of our yard was through a wooden staff and ticket working system for trains to the east of Railton whilst a different metal electric staff system was used to the west of Railton.

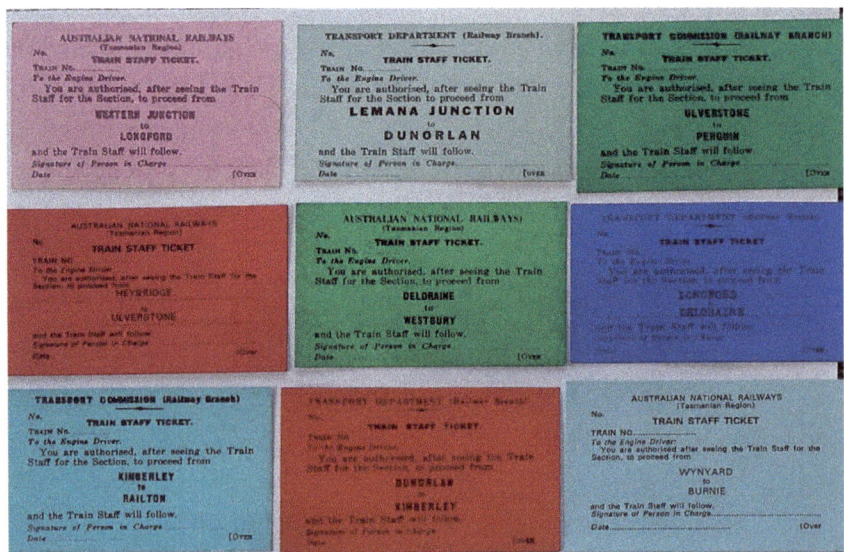

GL76 consignment note
(courtesy Kyle Stennings collection)

Train Staff tickets
(Courtesy David Payne)

It was not a terminal depot but an intermediate station where trains stopped on their way through, were added to or reduced and sent on further. The exception to this was the Goliath Cement train that had end terminals at both Railton and Devonport.

A level crossing was just some fifty metres away from the building and a lot of care was needed to shunt over the crossing. It was dangerous for motorists as they needed to cross over three tracks in the space of thirty metres. They don't always show regard for safety around any level crossings and many road vehicle collisions took place.

As a train cleared the line at the crossing, motorists would move on over with the crossing signal lights still operating and suddenly being confronted by another train on an adjacent line. Whenever trains were operating on the southern tracks we would physically man the crossing to halt the vehicles until all train movements were completed. Many times motorists would see the train movements and still make a decision to cross disregarding our directions anyway.

This behaviour most likely triggered my desire to do whatever I could in my career to improve level crossing safety awareness. I have always wondered why was it necessary to have tracks running both sides of the station. Surely planning could have been better?

Shunting wagons was not a simple thing to do. Care needed to be taken at all times. A string, of say, twenty wagons coupled together would create a lot of slack movement. When not correctly connected violent slack action occurs out on the track and a high derailment possibility is created. The wagons essentially ricochet off each other. Much care also needs to be taken as the shunter is standing in the dangerous position between the rails and the wagon buffers. Once the wagons are connected the shunter climbs back over the wagon buffers to the relatively safe ground trackside.

Wagon coupling links

Wet weather shunting was even more dangerous. Insecure footing was always an issue and wet weather gear was apt to catch on any nuts and bolt protrusions. The gear was very cumbersome particularly for that type of job. The buffers in particular seemed to think they had a given right to grab the coat every time you climbed over them. While wagons were being pushed and snatched by the loco and train consist it's not the time to fall, slip or get caught up.

With the exception of Terry Crisp's arm muscle getting pinched and badly bruised I never witnessed an injury to shunters while shunting. It was clearly very dangerous but it must be said that luck would have played a huge role. Current shunting procedures have come far to ensure safety.

Chapter Fourteen: Things in the night

After eighteen months I moved out of the single man's quarters and began travelling each day to work from Dunorlan. I purchased the quarters from the company as they were deemed surplus. With helpers, I dismantled them and trucked them up to the Great Lake. I reassembled them and they became my first of many shacks there. I loved the fishing in the area and building shacks there seemed a logical thing to do from a fishing and entrepreneurial point of view.

One time I enlisted the help of my brother-in-law Ron Cooper, who was married to Maureen, to drive dad's very old solid Bedford truck. It was old and tired from years of bushbashing for firewood with dad, but was of tough construction. The drive up the Lake Highway with its gravel and corrugated surface was painfully slow. It was loaded to the hilt which never helped either. On board was everything including the kitchen sink. It had flooring, windows, doors, galvanised water tanks, roofing materials and it probably looked as if someone was leaving home with everything they owned.

It was about nine o'clock at night and the road was foggy and had a dismal atmosphere as we climbed higher in altitude. The truck's headlights were dim at best and much concentration was needed to follow the narrow road. Ron and his brother, Greg, in the truck were in front going and myself and my other enlisted helper Rodney, were following behind in my HQ Holden. As we were driving at a snails pace an idea crept into my head. The Fairy Glade area has an eerie sense about it. It has overhanging low trees and the misty foggy night was brilliant for my plan.

I swapped the driving over to Rodney and he got me right up close behind the truck as it laboured up the hill at around ten kilometres an hour. It was easy to slip out the passenger side door and run up to the back of the truck. I climbed up the tailboard and crept between, over and around, the loading of timber and materials. As I neared the cabin of the truck I lowered myself down and slithered across the roof. It was of solid steel so my presence on there went undetected. With the misty fog and dim lights probing the gloomy road ahead, I actually allowed myself a chuckle even before the event occurred. The roof of the old Bedford was slightly curved toward the front so I hooked my boots into the railing behind the cabin and flopped my limp body down over the windscreen. My top half slapped onto the windscreen and my arms and head were facing the occupants fully from the view inside. For all money it sounded and appeared that a man's body had just fallen out of the drizzling night sky and crashed into the windscreen. Ron's foot hammered the brake pedal and the truck lurched to a shuddering stop. Ron's door remained shut as he was rigid in fright, but his brother's door was instantly flung open and he was out of there. Greg actually ran crashing into the roadside scrub in the dark in an effort to escape the death-like scene. I slid the rest of my body down the windscreen and onto the bonnet, and it wasn't until I was standing in their headlights in the drizzling mist that they recognised me. Ron wanted to kill me. Greg took some convincing to come back out of the scrub and declared he would not sleep that night and would never forget the experience.

It was one of my best pranks and Rodney and I laughed all the way to the Great Lake.

Another incident at the shack in Tod's Corner area of Great Lake occurred during it's construction. The helpers of the day had hooked up the trailer and went to the lake edge to gather shingle while I stayed behind at the shack to break up a lot of the larger sized rocks with a sledgehammer. The breaking down of the rocks and application of shingle smoothed out the rough stony driveway around the shack. As I began sledgehammering the larger rocks I got into a smooth swinging rhythm. I was swinging and breaking then moving slowly forward and swinging away again, when an almighty blow to my forehead laid me out unconscious. The shingle party pulled up just as I was coming to. They rushed over to help me up and asked what had happened. Blood was oozing from my forehead and an instant egg-sized lump and bruise was there. I replied that I didn't know, but it was decided that the sledgehammer had caught in the clothesline wire and careered back into my forehead. I was fortunate to be only knocked out as had it connected with my temple I would have been in more serious trouble.

The shackbuilding at the lakes was a way to escape from the railway work and brought much pleasure to fishing trips. I would quote for building demolition jobs, and if successful, then apply to the Railway company for a couple of weeks annual leave. The leave would cover for the estimated time frame to complete the demolition. I would sell off the unwanted materials from the demolished house or buildings and the rest I would keep as needed to build the shacks. I did scores of demolitions all along the coast and built four shacks at various locations on Great Lake. The demolition work was arduous and with the shack building in the sometimes inhospitable weather of the Central Plateau, it was a relief to get back to my normal job on the railway.

Chapter Fifteen: Change Coming

A new state of the art railway station was built about one kilometre west of our old Railton one.

It had a rail yard consisting of two straight loops and a main. A log loading track as well as the obligatory spur line out to the Cement Company. We had a flat yard with no curves in it. Bliss!! The new yard more importantly allowed for the Cement company's expansion of its quarry works. The relocation of the yard also got us away from the dreaded level crossings on the main street.

New Yard at Railton

The new yard with a small number of tracks which were longer and straight was ideally suited to the new freight pathway for the rail industry. Heavier and longer trains were made up of bulk containers, logs, superphosphates, cement, acid, bulk dangerous goods tankers, clay tankers, coal and timber. Gone were the less than container loads. There was no more mail, small goods, parcels, furniture, beer and the need for many station staff. A revolution in rail transport was fast occurring in Tasmania. Without doubt we also lost the human touch of the community through which trains now travelled.

The new yard was certainly a shunter's dream. It boasted complete end to end yard lighting on poles that lit the entire place up like it was daylight. We had new ballasted tracks with level blue metal walk ways, and it was dry underfoot. The old yard of mud in winter and dust in summer was a thing of the past.

New electric switches at each end of the yard allowed for them to be switched over from a panel in the station. Signals went from semaphore poles to turning a knob for electric coloured lights to admit trains. It became a much more hospitable place to work for a myriad of reasons. It was much less physical.

It didn't change the fun times that we created at work, in actual fact it allowed more time for it.

A new loading ramp was built for Blenkhorn's trucks to reverse up and dump their bulk loading of lime into our open topped wagons. The ramp was formed from crushed rock and metal and made to an appropriate height. This ramp and I came to grief one day. I had asked Alan, the assistant station master if he would like a lift home for lunch in my flash second hand Hillman Hunter sedan. A little beauty of a car she was and never gave me any trouble. It was furnished with luxurious plush bucket front seats.

It was approaching his lunch time so my timing needed to be right. He had to have exactly one hour for lunch and not a second less. He accepted my offer and duly settled in the passenger seat of my prized vehicle.

"This is nice" he commented as I sped off down the yard towards the yard exit. I said, "Hang on Alan we are taking a detour."

Instead of turning toward the exit I drove straight at the new ramp's side wall. I hit it at speed just as Alan's fingernails clamped into the soft dashboard lining. The angle created a wild sideways lift and we went up over the wall at speed. We both hit our heads on the roof and were jolted around violently. The front stone tray hit first and the too steep of an angle crumpled it up but the speed propelled us and finally the vehicle jolted to a stop perched precariously on the wall edge. We had bottomed out as we crunched on the top and my poor Hillman was stuck amid a cloud of dust and blue metal. We were stranded there with the front wheels off the ground. It all was over in about five seconds. Alan was quite shaken up and couldn't believe what just happened. He opened his door and got out carefully as the car was teetering on the edge. He still walked home for lunch, but I doubt he had much of an appetite.

The damage to the Hillman was extensive. Panels were pushed in, the bottom of the door sills were out of shape, it had a badly bent tail shaft along with buggered universal joints. The vehicle had to get towed and was put aside in the yard till repairs could be done. It was a massive miscalculation of speed and angles, but a hell of a hoot with Alan on board.

Another Hillman Hunter moment was when I was hooning into the yard when returning back from up the street. Heading around the corner in the yard and towards the station I spotted a trainee shunter walking toward the station. The road surface was blue metal that had a fine covering on top. Apparently it was also quite loose in terms of traction. I drove up behind him with a bit of speed and had intended to scare him into thinking I was out of control. When I got close and applied the brakes my tyres got no traction in the loose metal. I cannoned straight into him. The next thing I knew he was clunking up across my bonnet with arms and legs flailing everywhere. He grabbed at my windscreen wipers as he disappeared up over the windscreen, across the roof and thumped down across the boot onto the roadway behind me. By this time I had come to a stop and with my heart in my throat, I rushed back to discover the chap picking himself up in a dishevelled state, but thankfully still alive. He limped around all day at work, but said nothing about what really happened. I never did that again.

Notwithstanding the dust from vehicle traffic in and out of the yard, the new yard brought a massive leap forward in efficiency and safety. A boom in freight transport was occurring and the rail industry was in a competition for it like never before.

Goliath output was burgeoning and containerised freight took over the landscape. Locomotives got bigger, wagons got bigger, tonnage increased and trains became longer. Two-way radios took over from the arm waving signalling. The shunters became less fit and were "in a better paddock" as they say.

The Tasman Limited was closed down, so the associated staff were relocated to other places and roles. It had suffered from falling passenger numbers over many years and with the growing number of family cars its relevance to people moving was diminishing as well. Lots of serious train buffs still lament the loss of the nostalgic journey through the countryside. Passing by people's backyards rather than the house fronts gave a person a somewhat differing view of the neighbourhoods. Stewardess' gave commentary on passing geographical points of interest as it swayed along, but its demise was inevitable in monetary terms.

Staff came and went as usual but recruitment was more about capabilities. The early years of taking anyone unemployed and wanting a job were gone.

Chapter Sixteen: Kevin Norris

Among the rapid changes then happening, a newcomer arrived at Railton in 1981, when Kevin Norris was posted to the station master role and we wondered, "who the hell is this?" and "where did they get him from?"

Kevin Norris started as a fencer on the railway constructing trackside fencing in conjunction with adjacent farmers. The railway generally supplied materials and the farmer did the work putting them up, but quite often it ended up around the other way depending on farmer negotiations. Back in the day it was accepted that it was a shared responsibility to keep stock out of the rail corridor as equal boundary owners. Kevin was a part of a dedicated fencing gang. I'm sure that current adjoining landowners do not get a bi-partisan approach to maintaining fences. It would be expected that owners do what they have to do to keep stock safely on their property. It's very fair to say though that on occasions trains have been known to wander into the farmer's paddocks too. In the main, stock stay where they are supposed to, but as fences get dilapidated or pressure for feed comes on, particularly in the winter, cattle wander the train line corridor.

Kevin's fencing was generally down south in the state between Hobart and Maydena on the Derwent Valley line. He also fenced as far as Conara on the south line. He progressed up to a special ganger in charge of a group of fettlers that were known as The Flying Gang. He moved from infrastructure into operational grades and started at Tunbridge. He later went on to be assistant station master at Wynyard and as stationmaster at Ross.

Railton had become a major player in the network and Kevin took to the responsibility like a duck to water. It sat easy with him. Mainly I believe it was because he was the new way of Stationmasters in that the authoritarian and stiff stick mentality was gone. He was an equal participant in the smooth and efficient running of the place and title meant little unless something went wrong. Kevin was a man who always had the buck stop with him and a lot of mateship and respect came with that. Not one of my prior bosses had gone in to bat for their staff as much as Kevin.

While operating porters and assistant station masters were still required, the hierarchy was becoming more and more irrelevant. We just ran the place like a big family with no diminishment of responsibility or accountability to the effort. It was a much friendlier place to work and all seemed to share equal roles. It would have been difficult to understand who was a boss and who wasn't. Kevin instigated that culture and to be fair it suited him as he had a natural penchant to be one of the lads.

Kevin's house at Railton

Kevin was living in Danny's old house opposite the station and still does to this day with wife, Sandra. It was always a laugh when Kevin would get on the direct line from the station to his house when he wanted to tell her something or ask her to go fetch something. It was like a personal hot line. He would hold the handset of the ancient apparatus and vigorously wind the handle. If Sandra happened to not answer, Kevin would curse and declare "They're never home when you need them" and whack the handpiece down with pursed lips. I never did know if he was serious, but I guess only Sandra knows that.

After several years, he became the Area Manager for the North West Coast and shortly after moved to the office of Manager of Transport Services in Launceston. He travelled each day and stayed residing in the same humble weatherboard cottage at Railton. That was Kevin.

Kevin was a great story teller and still is. It wouldn't matter if he told you the same story three times in three years, it would still be delivered word for word and with the same gusto. I recently chatted with Kevin and the stories still flowed....

The 1967 bushfires decimated the south of the state and the Hobart Brewery burned down. Beer was being transported to Hobart from Launceston by both road and rail. Wagons were in short supply as many were being used for transporting stockfeed and other necessities from all parts of the state.

One particular train carrying beer had some flat top wagons and it arrived at Tunbridge station in the midlands region on its way south. I inspected the wagon's loadings due to reports of a strong smell of alcohol and discovered that the ropes holding the precious cargo had become loose and many cartons had collapsed and a large number of beer bottles were broken. The train controller of the day duly instructed the train's guard, Bob Seward and I to salvage all unbroken bottles onto the platform and re-tie the ropes and despatch the train. The salvaged bottles were placed into the Tunbridge storeroom under lock and key. There were many hundreds of bottles salvaged with just as many broken still piled in the wagon.

While re-tying the ropes around a damaged handrail, Bob pulled on it and the rail snapped off and sent him flying backwards to land in the pile of broken bottles. Bob's hands were lacerated badly and blood gushed everywhere from severed veins. I grabbed some twine used for parcel tying and made a tourniquet at both his elbows. I rang the local policeman who sped to the scene and took Bob to Oatlands and then on to Hobart hospital. Bob's hands were a mess afterwards and full use was never regained.

Also, while I was working at Maydena I was deliberately shut inside an EGX type box wagon. With me inside, the train was sent on to Westerway up the Derwent Valley Line where I was let out and taken by a pre-arranged car back to Maydena. It was a dark and empty box wagon and very rough to be in. It was a worry as I could not tell where I was or when I would be let out.

One time at the Wynyard station I was in my office and a wagon sped past the station by itself. Apparently Russell Holland, the shunter, was "fly" shunting a wagon. The phone was ringing and thinking someone else was catching the wagon, he went to answer the phone. No one caught the wagon so it subsequently ran past the station, through a locked gate and out onto the Wynyard Airport tarmac.

The train track actually traversed the airport runway and out the other side in a westerly direction. Obviously when planes were landing and taking off the rail access gates were shut against rail traffic. The problem was a runaway rail wagon had no regard for gates and luckily no planes were around at the time.

Kevin Norris.

DP carriages crossing Wynyard airport
(courtesy of Weston Langford)

While Kevin was my boss at Railton we had the funniest of times. We often played football out in the station yard driveway. Kevin, in his day, was a decent country footballer.

Cricket was also played on the platform almost every day. The ball, if caught off the station wall, was out and also if it went over the last rail of the back road track on the full. Alan Foster, while not partaking in the game, always took a standing position in the doorway so as to watch the comings and goings of batsmen. He would just ease back inside if the smashed ball headed his way. Although only a tennis ball was used at a distance of twenty feet it was still going to hurt. He took great pleasure at weaving back successfully into the doorway without being struck and giggled at each successful evasion. His head swivelled and he was ever-watchful, like a meerkat peeking from a burrow. One day he copped a full and lusty blow on the nose. Amid cries of, "Deliberate!! "Deliberate, I say!!" he retreated with deflated ego.

Electric staff columns

Chapter Seventeen: Pranks to die for

One really awful prank was to place detonators on the track whilst someone was shunting. I well remember the day they did it to me. Detonators were used to warn drivers out on the track of a danger ahead. They were placed – three at ten metres apart – and were detonated by wheel contact of the locomotive. The driver would then pull the train up safely in advance of the problem. The detonators were secured in the station safe and had thin metal straps to fold down around the rail to hold them in place.

Detonator

The perpetrators in my case were never ascertained but quite a number were aware it was going to happen. It was my first and only detonator episode.

It happened while shunting on the mainline just down from the station platform. I gave the driver the signal to ease up and stepped between the rails. Standing between the rails and buffers, there was only enough room to move forward and back a little. The awareness of wagon movement is prudent so as not to be injured as you are unable to quickly extricate from that space. As the wagon moved slightly the detonator exploded under the wheel and my heart leapt into my throat. I was thinking, "What the bloody hell?" It went off like a gunshot. It bloody nearly scared me to death. It was a frightening noise in itself let alone the fact I was standing in the danger zone. When my fright settled I still didn't realise what had happened until I heard the sounds of raucous clapping and laughter from the platform. I peeked out from between the wagons and there were six to eight people on the platform revelling in their success. My mind went into response mode. I wanted to make the mongrels pay. I collapsed on the side of the track clutching my leg and chest. I put on a fantastic theatrical performance. It was about to become my best yet. I staggered to my feet hunched over in apparent pain and distress, but still the clowns on the platform chortled and high fived. I had more to show them. With me staggering and clutching, I painfully lurched up onto the platform and went into the crib room. Doubt starting to seed in their minnow brains. Alone in the crib room I quickly unbuttoned my shirt and splashed tomato sauce on my chest. It was a mess, but I needed to sell this act well. With a dishevelled look and flapping shirt half off me I let out a scream and staggered back out onto the platform collapsing in front of them all. I turned over on my back and let my blood red arm and hand fall from my shirt. My yelling in pain and the sight of apparent metal damage from the detonator and the pretend blood had them rushing to my aid. It was a performance of great conviction. Some rushed to the platform edge with ashen faces to dry reach and others by my side were convinced that an ambulance was needed. In a minute flat, their fun and laughter had turned to shock and horror. I let them soak in that for a minute and then hopped up to my feet and said, "Take that you flipping mongrels" or words to that effect.

Some forty or so years later it was still my best comeback. The dead snakes placed in workbags or fishplates to add weight to them paled into insignificance that day. No one ever detonated anyone again.

I have previously mentioned flying wagons when shunting. "Flying" was a term used to describe a shunt movement which was allowed back in the past, but with modern shunting rules is now banned. It is done when a wagon is hooked on the rear of the locomotive and allows for the wagon to be "flown" from the rear of the locomotive to it's front. Then being on the front of the loco, it would simply be pushed to the required place.

Just prior to approaching the switches, the shunter who was laying prone over the buffers on the wagon or loco would signal the driver by the dropping of his free hand while hanging on with the other. On the sighting of the hand drop the driver would reduce speed causing the trailing wagon to bunch up, enabling the shunter to lift the link separating the wagon. The shunter, while still laying over the buffer holding on tight to the loco rail or wagon, would with his free hand, signal to the driver to speed up. The driver would then increase the throttle and go ahead to open the gap between it and the still travelling wagon. When the loco was clear of the switches another shunter would throw the switches over and allow the loose approaching wagon to be diverted and run itself into the siding. The shunter that was laying over the loco buffer had in the meantime got off the now stopped loco to catch and hand brake the loose wagon to a stop in the siding. There was clearly a high element of danger, but to the shunters it was an adrenaline high. It also saved a damn lot of running around after wagons and shunting work.

Although no one ever got hurt in my time, it was a given that as safety improvement became part of the industry "flying wagons" was always going to get banned.

On one occasion we were "flying" a wagon and Max was owed a prank by me, and the day had come to pay him back. It was his turn to lay over the loco buffer and control the flying shunt movement and signals . My job was to turn the switch. All was going well as he separated the link and the loco sped up to open the gap. The loco went past me with Max in place and hanging onto the X loco handrail. He yelled out, "turn the switches."

X locomotive handrails where Max sought refuge

As the loco went by me I looked at Max with my arms crossed, smiling. I allowed the switch to remain the same which meant the wagon coming along loose by itself was still going up the same track as the loco. Max's eyes widened as he realised his predicament. The loco stopped as normal but the wagon was clearly going to crash into it with Max still there. His decision making was patchy. For one second he thought of throwing himself backwards onto the ballast but decided to climb the loco face handrail instead.

    The wagon hit the now stationary loco so hard it bounced back up the track some fifteen to twenty metres. The drivers in the loco were also shaken up by the impact. While pleased for getting one back on Max it did cross my mind that the wagon could have easily sprung up off the buffers and climbed up the loco face where Max had taken sanctuary. I did not do that again.

Chapter Eighteen: Latrobe

About eleven kilometres north of Railton was the town of Latrobe. Latrobe Railway Station was without doubt like all early stations, the central hub of the town. Almost all activity centred about the station. Pulpwood, potatoes and everything else produced in the region was transported by rail, along with all needs and requirements of the town coming in by train. As a consequence the town businesses and buildings were concentrated close to the rail depot.

So many people these days complain that train lines go through their town when in fact the railhead was there and the people actually built around it. Now many years later this is lamented by most residents. The now much longer trains with massive locomotives of 2000 horsepower with seemingly ceiling scratching high pitched whistles became very annoying to most. Yes, it is said some get used to it and there are those with nostalgic love of them, but in the main most residents wish they were not there.

Latrobe main street – adjacent to old station site

How attitudes change with changing circumstances! The town is bustling with cars and tourists on the streets, oblivious to the era past. Transport to them now was having two cars in the driveway. Having a train station in the town was an unnecessary impost.

The bypassing of Latrobe occurred in 1983. The track was cut from the western side of the Mersey river and straight-lined more or less to re-join the original main just near the Ballyhoo Creek bridge west of Latrobe.

Remains of Ballyhoo creek rail bridge

A portion of the original rail corridor is now part of that town's Teddy Sheean Walk. It begins at the former level crossing in the town centre and is dedicated to commemorating Sheean's sacrificial manning of his ship's gun to fire at enemy aircraft during WW2. Strapped to the *Armidale's* gun, he was still firing as it slowly slipped under a bloodied sea. The Victoria Cross was awarded to Teddy after seventy odd years of efforts to have his bravery recognised.

Teddy Sheean Walk at Latrobe

Chapter Nineteen: Phillip Moore

Phillip Moore was already at the old station at Railton when I arrived as the lad porter. We became good friends and were seen as the leading shunters in terms of skillsets. I soon learned that from sheer experience he was a long way in front and as such I afforded him every respect.

Phillip started work at Spreyton station in 1968, so some five years before I even left school. Spreyton, like lots of other outlying stations also incorporated the post office duties. He was only there for four months and then transferred to Latrobe in unusual circumstances as an eighteen year old. Latrobe's lad porter had been dismissed for stealing boxes of Wagon Wheels, of the chocolate confectionary type, from a customer's order. Station master Len Herbert was a very strict disciplinarian and the lad porter needed to go. A silly act of theft from a customer never had a breath of a chance for him to stay employed. So Phillip replaced him and after a time progressed to the position of staff working porter. He eventually progressed up to fully qualified shunter ranks. He reflected on the things that happened at Latrobe and Railton during his time.

I had two separate stints at Latrobe and you know it was hard work back then so we broke it up with the fun of setting your workmates up for a fall. Heaps of crazy stuff went on.

One time a driver of a train that had stopped up at Railton had spotted a snake curled up soaking in some sun next to the track. He got out of the cab and despatched the snake and took it on board the locomotive with him. After shunting, he drove the train down to us at Latrobe. His authority to travel down was administered by possession of a metal staff. The staff was placed in a leather pouch that is affixed to a metal hoop so as to pass it easily out the window to the station master. This was particularly handy if the train was passing through non-stop. The handing over of the staff relinquished the train's authority out on the track and it then came under the station master's yard authority. A commotion erupted when the hooped staff was scooped over the outstretched arm of a staff member on the platform and the four feet long black snake was wrapped around it. The station master had no time for such shenanigans and all concerned were spoken to.

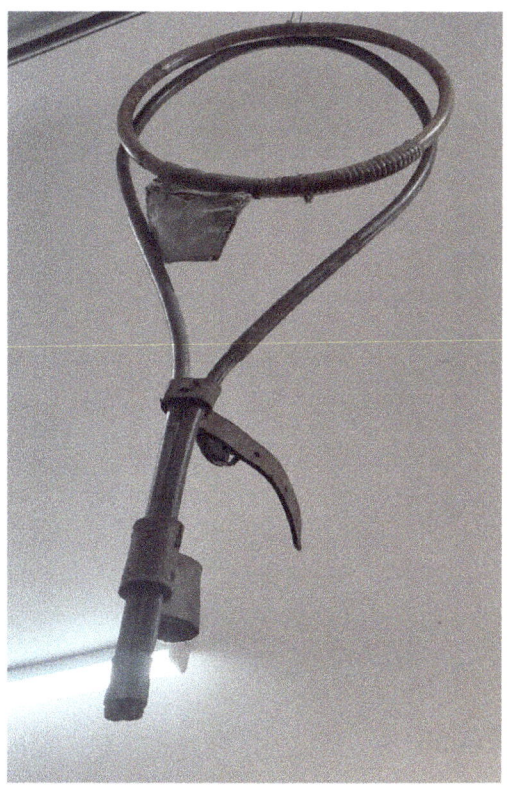

Old electric staff hoop

Another day a trainee porter got me involved in a discussion about the various types of fireworks and their potency. I told him I bought some once that would go off underwater, which was roundly denounced as bull crap. I asked him to buy this certain type of cracker and bring them to work and we would see. The next day we got in the toilet and I lit a handful of crackers all at once and dropped them into the toilet bowl. The toilet bowl shattered into a hundred pieces and water went everywhere. He took off and wanted no part of it. He was very scared of Len's reaction and was only a beginner on the job. Len knew of the young fella's passion for letting off firecrackers and he knew that he would be blamed for sure.

While I was young at Latrobe I was with a bunch of young guys that hung around each other in town. We went out on the grog one Friday night and had a beer barrel, but couldn't finish it off. So, the next morning I invited the gang to fetch it down to the rail station and we sorted out the remaining contents. The day was uneventful otherwise, thankfully.

On the last day of the running of the Tasman Limited there were celebrations at every station throughout its journey and we were no different. It was July 1978 and some of us bought Coca-Cola cans to drink, but they were topped up with a little rum to celebrate the occasion. Just by chance the traffic inspector arrived, revelling in the celebrations with the public and dignitaries that thronged the stations that day. We also noted the rail company detective, but it deterred us not. We continued walking around with our loaded up cans and chatted bare-faced with the bosses. We were particularly pleased to pull the wool over the eyes of the detective. He was a fully paid permanent detective on the railway and we giggled our way through the day as to how easy it was.

I went up to Railton for a few years as a Leading Shunter. I was sort of the senior shunter with that role.

Back in those early days we still carried coffins by rail. Some were empty returning to the funeral parlour, but often they actually contained a body. If someone had passed in Hobart and needed to be interred at Railton or Sheffield for example, the occupied coffins were in box wagons and loaded there by funeral staff and on arrival unloaded by funeral staff

at the destination station. Station personnel were not allowed to touch them. One day an empty coffin was unloaded from the wagon and placed in the storeroom for collection. It happened to be placed alongside the stack of tarpaulins. Knowing that super phosphate wagons were shortly to be covered by tarps for transport, a shunter rolled himself up in a tarp and when the lad porter came in to pick one up, the shunter began moaning and groaning in mournful tones muttering, "let me out", "let me out". The lad porter took flight out of the storeroom and declared to the stationmaster that he was not cut out for this job and was never seen again.
    Phillip Moore

Phillip was a leader among shunting ranks and for most of us at the new station he seemed to be around forever. He gave me a nickname of "Ralph" and to this day I don't know why. To his dismay it never stuck or resonated with anyone else at work, but to his credit still calls me that every single time he sees me. I think it was possibly to do with the character on the television show, Happy Days. The character talked a hell of a lot and I think it was his cynical attempt at saying I liked a chat too. Out of respect I have never asked or protested the nickname.

    Phillip, Max and I always got on well but we really were so different to each other that it seemed impossible. Max was always held at arms length because you just couldn't tell when he was on your side.

    Max and I once got mixed up in a derailment incident and each blamed the other. The traffic inspector of the day, Fred Brazier, drove up from Devonport to Railton in order to determine the culprit. We both had very different views on what had happened. Fred's fierce finger-pointing style didn't really bring about a resolution. Max, being the character he was and always on the front foot, declared to Fred, "Let's just suppose Ralph's story is true." I couldn't believe my ears as

Max had never ever called me that and Fred immediately cut off Max from talking further. Fred told Max that he didn't believe him and he would be summarily issued with a form 109a, which was a warning from the brass and a misdemeanour charge.

Phillip Moore, who just by chance was listening in on the conversation behind the door, commented to me as I came out of the room, "Let's just suppose Ralph's story is true." He knew as well as I did it was my fault and that I'd lied like hell. The phrase thereafter lived on.

Getting wet at work was easy enough being an outdoor job. It was however made worse by people lying in wait on top of the station roofs. When walking up the platform it was always a good idea to watch and listen for a person on the roof with a bucket of water to dump on you. A horrible thing it is to have a dunking at the very start of a shift. It was a good idea to have some spare clothes in our lockers. Phillip Moore was the worst culprit for this by far.

There was lots of other ducking for cover situations while working there as well. When the twice daily blasting in the Goliath Quarry occurred the rocks would sometimes reach our yard. An alarm would sound signalling that their blasting was about to commence and we would hide behind wagons for protection. It was common for large chunks to rain through the trees and down into the new, much closer yard.

Chapter Twenty: Ferrets Working On The Railway

Rabbits had been making a bountiful comeback over a number of years. Although not in the plagues of my younger years, they certainly were returning on a renewed path. They seemed to have built a resilience to the Myxomatosis virus that was set among their populations through the 1950's. Carried by fleas and mosquitos it wreaked havoc, but natural immunity was starting to develop and they were proving resistant to it. The rabbit populations were also flayed by the developed RCD (rabbit calicivirus disease). Both were biological controls. The rabbits were overcoming these threats to their existence and pockets of populations began emerging. The rough geographical triangle encompassing my old stomping ground of Deloraine, Mole Creek and Kimberley was one such pocket of renewal and I set about revisiting my childhood passion. I bought two young doe ferrets and with a little maintenance on my nets and boxes I was set, and basking in anticipation.

My ferreting gear

Whenever I was on night shifts and the weather permitted, I would go ferreting during the day. In my teenage years I saw it as an opportunity to wag school and make pocket money, but my employer would not be as accepting as my teachers. I never did wag work to go ferreting, but I certainly used shift work to my advantage so there was a sort of co-existence.

The rabbit hunting ferret

Night shift commenced at 10pm and went through to 6am. When knock off time came around I was reasonably well rested because of the trusty single mattress squirrelled away in the storeroom. Sometimes the train would be outside the door and a short pop on the whistle stirred me from slumber. I would stagger out and shunt the train, depart it and quickly compress the mattress back to sleep. Sometimes I could get blocks of sleep of two and three hours.

At 6am I would knock off and feeling well rested, drive out to my old rabbiting grounds of Red Hills and Lemana

Junction. My vehicle at this time was a 720 dual cab Datsun ute. It carried a pair of ferrets in their boxes, ten string nets and eight wire nets, along with a couple of sack bags to carry the rabbits. I also transported a mesh crate, predominately built from lightweight materials with lots of air flow opportunity.

I would park the ute in the shade whenever possible. The rabbits piled on top of each other which caused them to suffocate so cool air and gaps were important because dead rabbits didn't make me any money. They had a stupid tendency to pile up on top of each other in the box even though there was plenty of open space all around them. The crate had a trapdoor fitted in the top so I could simply take the live rabbit from the net and drop it in through the trapdoor. It would be free to run around live in the box for later retrieval. When I had a good day on the rabbits the cage would have sixty or seventy in it. The heat generated in the cage from their bodies was surprising.

Usually, and more or less dependent on the heat of the day a full size potato sack would only hold about twelve rabbits because of suffocation risk.

Around 4pm I would pack up and return home with my bounty. I firstly would put away my ferrets to their cage and feed and water them. I would have a shower and a feed myself and go to bed for about three hours prior to heading to work at 10pm again. The wearing nature of patches of sleep and the hard work of ferreting usually called for only two or three days ferreting midweek during night shifts.

On arrival at work I would park my utility on the platform and set about my work on the rabbits. First, I would lay out a tarp on the storeroom floor. After checking on train schedules and making sure everything was clear for a while, I would start on the rabbits in the crate in the back of the vehicle. I would take each rabbit from the cage via the trapdoor and despatch it and skin it. The dressed rabbit was then hung by its leg on nails that I had set about 30 centimetres apart in the lovely varnished storeroom racks and shelving. When about a dozen or so were done I would transfer them to the main office desks and benches. With often sixty full sized rabbits done, the storeroom looked like an abattoir or a murder scene of Hollywood proportions. Ian and Alan's desks were covered in rabbit carcases and apart so as to be allowed to set. The storeroom was looking shocking. Rabbit heads, legs, guts and skins were strewn all over the tarp. There is also an amazing amount of blood from the killing of so many rabbits. It was probably an unnerving sight to city folk, but to a hardened country kid it meant little. To me it was just a mess to clean up. I would gather all the bits and pieces into a bag and carry it across the tracks into the bush opposite the station. It was with a smile that I noticed that crows had taken up permanent residency in that area. It had become a ready-made smorgasbord for them.

    I pulled the tarp out onto the platform, hosed it down and rolled it up until next time. The trains came and went and this rabbit work was fitted in between them. Then it was time to sleep. Out with the trusty mattress and with no rocking I would be out like a light.

    Before finishing work at 6am, I would box up all the set rabbits in cardboard boxes and tape them securely. On leaving work I would drop the boxes of rabbits off at Boxhall's shop in the main street of Railton for transport to arranged butcher shops in Launceston by the Redline Coach Service.

    I then drove back up to Lemana Junction and it started all over again. It was another day and different rabbits. I sure as hell earned my money over the two to three days.

    One morning the relieving station master Alwyn Parker came to work early for some reason at about 5am and walked into the office to find dressed rabbits filling all the desks and bench tops. He was impressed with that but upon walking into the storeroom with the mess not yet cleaned, lurched back outside dry reaching and gagging over the platform edge. He was a tad upset by the sight.

100 dressed rabbits

Another group that got caught up in my rabbiting were the guys that came up to Railton from Devonport each day to do maintenance and minor wagon repairs in our yard. They would inspect any rolling stock and fix any defective brake rigging gear.

One chap had a penchant for taking magazines from my workbag. It did grate me a little and any suggestion from me that he should ask before delving into my bag was just met with a scoff. One day I took to work a rabbit trap. On placing my bag on the bench I put the rabbit trap into my bag so that it sat on top. I placed a magazine down the side of the bag and allowed just one page to drape over the trap. Anyone touching the page would discover the trap and with a little imagination realise that had it been set they would have been the owner of a handful of broken fingers. I was dobbed in to the boss by someone seeing me set it up. I duly got a dressing down but never again was my bag interfered with.

Rabbit trap (workbag protector)

Chapter Twenty One: Switch-It

During day shifts that ran from 8am to 4pm, unlike in the early days, there were many hours to kill. Phillip Moore and I would play a card game called Switch-it or as some call the game, Twos and Threes. It's a simple game really and not one normally associated with adults. The way we played it at the Railton railway station was like no other place. We would play for many hours and it became legend among staff and train crews along the entire North West Coast. Kevin Norris became intoxicated with it. He would insist that all shunting and required work was done first, but after that it was really on in the Switch-it stakes.

The game is more complicated in pairs so instead of Phillip Moore and myself playing each other as it was in early days, we paired up together to play anybody in a pairs challenge. We always won. After many weeks of no-one being able to beat us at such a straightforward and simple game it became a challenge to knock us off our high and mighty perch. There was fierce competition to get in line to beat us.

The office would have the normal non-players like Alan and Phillip Foster watching with craning necks. It was mind boggling to watch grown men lining up in ever-hopeful expectation of becoming the new champions. The potential suitors lined up eagerly then slunk away from the table as depressed as a child that received no gifts at Christmas-hurt! Their annoyance clearly palpable as they relinquished their seats. All it did was fuel heightened tension about how it was possible for these two shunters to always win. The game was played in front of the most calculating and watchful audience. The next in line were always checking for signs of cheating or some signal skulduggery. But alas, it all seemed to be just a matter of skill and luck.

The hurt became more powerful as the weeks turned into months of playing the game against all comers. No-one tried to show it outwardly in case it affected their concentration. There was however, the occasional kicking over Ian's paper bin as they left the table and the muttered cursing upon the door slamming as they stormed out. The fervour that built up around it was just unbelievable.

Word spread and soon gang road vehicles were turning up to play. Three or four men would feign checking on the train whereabouts to join in. One gang leader in particular took serious exception to defeat. In a fit of unbridled rage, he grabbed all the cards and threw them out the station window. While we were still in shock at his petulance we heard a revving of a truck outside. We looked out the window to see his ganger's truck driving back and forth over the cards.

Train drivers of the shunting crew roster would eagerly await their turn as well. Switch-it dominated the workplace. I think because Kevin was involved it sort of gave it the green light to grow even more. It was played anywhere from one hour to five hours every day. There were times when we came close to losing and that just added petrol to the fire.

Challengers started to wane, so Phillip and I invented a pretend Switch-it trophy. It hung on an imaginary nail up on the office wall. As challengers sat down to play one of us would point to the wall and say, "The famous, much sought after Switch-it trophy is up for grabs." Players just accepted that it was there and it was on the line to win. We milked it for all it was worth. Upon losing, players would declare, "We will be back to get you tomorrow." It was a laugh, but deadly serious.

Sometimes the pairs would blame each other for the loss and swap partners. Kevin was so funny to watch playing it. If nothing else he was happy to display determination. Gritted teeth and pursed lips, eyes darting from player to player and with a clenched fist slam his want-to-be winning card down. Sometimes they were winners, but just not when it mattered. The spectators were waiting for a fuse to blow. It was close many times. Everyone wanted to watch us get beat. Such was the passion.

Well, up until the writing of this book only Phillip Moore and I know why we were the best and it was so simple, because we cheated the best. While playing pairs we roughly knew what cards each of us had in our hands. In some cases we knew exactly.

If we had a jack in our hand we would have it sitting proud of the other cards. They sat up only couple of millimetres so as not to be obvious. All other cards were perfectly in line across the top. The jack card was very handy as it caused the next opponent to miss a turn and therefore increase the chances of us to play our last card. Where it really hurt our opponents was if we had multiple jacks. We could keep our opponents at bay and allow us free swings to get out to victory.

As well as that, whenever we held a two or a three card we would hold the cards in our hands with either two or three fingers at the front. Whacking a two or three on an opponent forced them to pick up that number of cards from the deck. If we held a number of them we could load them up before skipping out as well.

The real clincher, though was our knocking system. If either of us was on a last card it required us to knock on the table to advise our opponents. If our last card was a heart suit we would knock once. If it was a diamond we would knock twice. If it were a spade we knocked three times. But to allay suspicion when we had a club suit we would knock excitedly a lot of times so fast that counting them was not possible. Knowing what suit each other had meant we could use a jack or an ace and even a two or three of that suit to assist us out of cards and win. It was a hoot. It wasn't fool proof, but damn close.

Then the unthinkable happened!

We lost!

We were beaten fair and square by a train crew up from Devonport. How, with all our cheating processes in place, we didn't know. Thousands of games were played over such a long time without loss. We were made get the imaginary shield down off the wall and present it to the victors. We never played the game again. It died that day as the incentive was gone, as was our coveted trophy to Devonport.

Phillip and I don't know if they cheated or not, but we hoped not because that would have been unfair we thought. To all those train crews and gangs we could say we are sorry for cheating and especially if it sent you home angry to your family. But we are not…it was so much fun.

Chapter Twenty Two: Crewing and the resurrection

Shunt crews were always a weird mix. The driver and his fireman would arrive at Railton by road from Devonport. They would perform the yard shunts with either a "V" class loco or sometimes an X loco. The "V" was stabled at Railton.

V class loco

The "V", at around 25 tonnes in weight and fitted with 204hp Gardner motors, was very capable of pulling long strings around in the yard. The British built diesel had been the forerunner that kickstarted the dieselisation of Tasmanian Government Railways (T.G.R). and four units arrived in the late 1940's, followed by several more in the early 1950's. Some modified models were built in the Launceston workshops. "V" locomotives were stationed at various depots around the state for shunting duties and withdrawn from service between 1983 and 1987. They were small and the cab space quite limited.

As with the pairing of all work crews that work in small confines, particular attention to compatibility needed to apply. Eight hours a day in a small locomotive cab that rattled and vibrated all the time would test one's friendship with their workmate. More often than not compatibility was excellent between crews and usually any fractious goings on were sorted in good time.

Sometimes when a crew were at odds with each other, the ill feeling transferred to us shunters. It would then be a long day for us. It seemed they would see us only when they wanted to. Any protestation from us would be met with the "well wave your bloody arms harder then" or "oh, sorry, we didn't see you."

Our eight hours was going to feel like ten hours. Any lateness of the train being marshalled for departure was always seen as the shunters fault bringing down the wrath of the stationmaster and no-one questioned the driver. Some of them thought of shunters as just ballast plodders.

There were many times that issues of incompatibility in the cab boiled over to a bit of physical push and shove. Most just simmered and over time would fizz out, but occasions of full on biffs did occur. A few never took a backward step. Any enquiry into these events by management, were usually met by stony silence.

One angry incident occurred when I tried to get Max into trouble. Whenever we went to the Goliath yard for shunting, the race was on to clamber up into the loco. This was because if you were last in you would have to get out to turn the switches at Goliath. It was a small thing to argue over, but it was particularly important in bad weather.

Max had got in first and took up the coveted position against the wall and therefore I was consigned the indignity of switch turner. Max was standing across the cab just quietly tossing a couple of pieces of ballast as I exited the cab to turn the switch. Before I got back in the cab I picked up a piece of ballast and concealed it in my hand. As it happened one of the drivers had a coffee sitting on the ledge and without anyone seeing I slipped the ballast into his mug. A minute later the driver took a mouthful of his coffee and the errant piece of ballast hit him in the teeth. He was shocked and spluttered the coffee out, along with the ballast. And Max, still tossing up his ballast pieces caught the full blame and wrath. The driver grabbed a shifter out of his bag and lunged at Max. The other driver and I grabbed at the enraged man as Max lit out the door in escape lest the word Sidchrome would be emblazoned on his forehead. Max (Marine, Motorcycles and Mobile Homes) knew I had set him up, but that was not the time to discuss it.

People came and went in the staffing at Railton. Phillip Moore was seconded to Devonport as a relieving supervisor. Kevin Norris by this time had become the Area Manager for the North-West coast.

Shunters became more mobile for a while as they were given cars to drive around from depot to depot; they could fill positions as required instead of being permanent depot shunters.

Many stations had no staff at all from an operational point of view, so the shunter would drive to meet the train at each location and perform the shunt. After the shunt it would be departed to the next location. The shunter then drove and waited for it and performed the shunt there as required and again departed the train. This would continue throughout the shift. A marked change had come over the shunter's role. They were mobile shunters.

Of course all the small outlying stations such as Hagley, Westbury, Exton, Lemana Junction, Dunorlan, Moltema and Kimberley were no longer manned. Across the state the same had occurred everywhere. There were many dozens of derelict and overgrown station platforms with the station buildings long since gone. These days the manned stations on the western line are Western Junction, Devonport and Burnie.

A derelict and empty Kimberley

One station that resisted closure for a time at least was the Penguin Railway Station. It is the only railway station that I know of that had diminished in trade and function, just like dozens before it, to be removed and then as if by magic reappear on the same site just like it was before!! Unusually this was twenty two years later.

A derelict and empty Lemana Junction

Original Penguin Station
(courtesy of Penguin History Group)

The original station welcomed its first train on 15th April 1901. They dealt with the bustle of pulpwood loadings and the massive piles of potato sacks to be loaded onto wagons for market in the bigger towns to the west and east. It was a busy place for many years. Later, a diminishing freight task and a changing landscape with roads and more vehicles using them saw many stations close. The worker's train ceased in 1962, and the Tasman Limited in 1978 and Penguin station itself closed in 1982.

A local prominent businessman, Mr Ron Gee, was anxious to see the building preserved rather than demolished. He purchased the entire building and transported it to his property, and there it sat for the next two decades.

The Penguin history group started to dream about the idea of it's return and over a period the chatter and fervour grew about it's reincarnation. Many stakeholders got together to make it happen, including Ron. The amount of work and effort to bring it back and re-site would have been huge. It stands in Penguin today as a symbol of resilience and community spirit; amid much fanfare and celebrations it was re-born on the 15th of April 2001, exactly one hundred years after it first opened.

The returned Penguin Station

Chapter Twenty Three: Moving Toward Train Driving

The big numbers at the larger stations created an atmosphere of camaraderie and family. However, no longer did the gangs call in and add some banter and their bit; no longer did the customers come; and no longer did the paper pushers ply their trade. The paperwork was sent via the atmosphere and centralised in Launceston instead of over Ian's and Alan's desks. What was also dying was the human interaction within the workplace. Some stations had become empty deserts and the quiet was only interrupted by the sound of a train passing through.

Massive numbers of fettlers were also lost from the gangs. Every five or ten kilometres there used to be a gang to tend that section with a few flying gangs or special gangs overlapping. Almost all were replaced with the arrival of huge packing machines.

Tamping machine
(courtesy of Kyle Stennings)

They could lift, cant and pack the track in a day which would take fifty men a month with picks and shovels. They did it all and the men were lost and obsolete. My dad would turn over in his grave in disbelief at the massive loss of jobs and mateship. Everywhere in the state the fettlers left or retired and were not replaced. Only a handful remained in the state in small isolated roles.

Operational staffing levels were being diminished as well and it was rapid. But, with the loss of humans came the loss of humanity. An 'every man for himself' attitude was leeching into the mentality of the workplace. As jobs became lesser in number the pressure to keep them became more important. Although it wasn't spoken about it was a reality that stealthily hung in the air.

Phillip Moore retired from the position of Supervisor at Devonport on the first of October 1993. He thanked me for the use of my single man's quarter's way back in those early days at the old station when I was a lad porter. Apparently when I was away for a day or two he would let himself in and using my bed entertain the girlfriends there. How could he do that and not say anything. The fiend!!

In due course I was seconded to the relieving operation's supervisor role. This role was expanded to include the operations of Devonport and Railton combined. Railton had succumbed like the rest. The coal trains and cement trains servicing Goliath were still going there, but that was about it; bulk commodity trains that required little or no shunting.

During my time at Devonport it was becoming increasingly obvious to me that it was imperative to become a driver. Both driver and shunter roles were very much the only ones available with any security. Even managerial roles were few in number. I decided that driving was where I needed to be. A shunter was outside in all weather, but the drivers were up in their nice warm cabs with more money. A no-brainer I thought. The problem was that everyone else thought the same. They could all see the writing on the wall.

The opportunity for a person to be lifted up onto the driver's roster opened up and the position of trainee driver was going at Devonport. I was beside myself with hope. So was everyone else. In the modern times the trainee driver opportunity was gold and people would kill for it. The subsequent landslide of applicants occurred and the process began. No shunter with any age wanted to footslog the yards anymore.

I was perceived by most as a frontrunner for the position, but that certainly didn't deter anyone from going hell for leather at it. My shunting history and the supervisory role, I believed would hold me in good stead.

Interviews for the role occurred over several days due to the large number of aspirants. The couple of weeks waiting for the result was painfully slow. Then the phone call came. I didn't get the job.

Admittedly I was in shock as my hopes were very high. I believed my experience and hard work would have seen me good, but it was not to be apparently. I received phone calls from managers in Launceston who also could not believe the result. I had to explain it to all and sundry, but I had no answer for them or me. I bade good luck to the Devonport shunter awarded the job and had to sit in my office in Devonport watching him ride by each day up in the locomotive. He had to be pleased with the result and fair enough. It was a bitter pill to swallow just the same.

Over the next few days I analysed it and wondered what went wrong as I pondered my future on the railway. After the supervisor role I guessed I was destined to footslogging as a shunter forever. My frustration was compounded by a friend in management who informed me I had come last in the interview panel's view. I thought, this is just bloody bullshit. I was at home one night still lamenting it. No doubt it impacted my family life as I felt very down and depressed for weeks when a phone call came like a bolt out of the blue.

On the other end of the phone was a senior manager who explained that he heard that I was never allowed to be given the job because I was seen as required as the supervisor. This information was first hand as the panel was discussing in his company about how that may be facilitated. The manager said if I really wanted the job there was an appeal process that I could go through that would cause the panel to re-interview the incumbent and me, to put a case for wrongful decision.

I am indebted to that person for telling me of that chance to appeal and for the courage of convictions to not allow something wrong to go by. He was also willing to be a witness to the apparent error of judgement.

I appealed the decision and consequently angst surrounded the Devonport Rail Yard for the next two weeks while the appeal case was heard. I was not a friend of anyone within the Devonport ranks, especially as I was a "foreigner" from Railton.

A magistrate was flown in from Melbourne and a new panel selected with the magistrate having the deciding vote. Both the incumbent and myself were transported in separate vehicles to Launceston for the hearing. It was a weird feeling.

The appeal was upheld and the incumbent was released back to shunter ranks and my train driving career began. My thanks never waned for that manager for his courage to set things right. And so from very meagre beginnings as a lad porter with Reginald at Dunorlan, I finally was a trainee locomotive driver.

Chapter Twenty Four: Finally Driving

I was paired up with Allan Hind. He was a skilled driver trainer and an affable type of guy that had a proven way of transferring his knowledge and experience across to any trainee. I was thrilled to be his partner.

In just a few months a real upheaval for the rail in Tasmania developed with talk of the state owned railway being sold out to a private enterprise. This upheaval was new and scary for us all.

Ownership changed for the railway when the consortium of Wisconsin Central of North America (the largest regional railway in North America) and Tranz Rail of New Zealand formed Australian Transport Network (ATN) and purchased the company. in 1997. Every employee was made redundant and then needed to re-apply for their jobs. It was a terrible time. Having worked so loyally for so many years and having to sit a series of interviews in order to get our jobs back was frightening. The age old rule that a job on the railway was a job for life had been summarily shattered. It was an even more daunting prospect for people that hadn't sat for a job interview in forty years. It became a dog-eat-dog situation between previous work mates. People would do anything in order to keep a job, make house payments, send kids to school and put food on the table.

The interviews were to be done over two stages and as it turned out, almost all got their jobs back. The new owners had the opportunity to be selective and place people where they wanted them. Weeks of rumours suggested that some employees would receive full time contracts and the rest would be only offered temporary jobs. It was even scarier not knowing until "D" day. My entire career was now on the line.

While on the locomotives as a trainee, the new owners began doing the interviews. I was interviewed twice which I thought was promising, but later realised it happened to everyone. I was hoping to keep my recently obtained trainee driver role. I lost a lot of sleep over it. Two children to raise and a mortgage to pay was a worry. I would not be alone in my anxiousness.

In scenes never before known to rail workers, our staff, including me, trudged into the office and awaited our fate. We each went in and received either a large or small envelope. It soon enough was known that a large envelope had a contract for a full time position whilst the small envelope had a six month temporary job offer in it. The rumours were true.

Allan Hind at the controls. (courtesy of Barbara Hind)

In a devastating blow to my trainer, Allan, received only a short term offer. I had received a full time offer of contract, but to accept it I was required to transfer to the Burnie depot. Devonport would soon be operationally closed. That was a shock to hear, but it became true and Devonport was soon almost silent and only a skeleton staff stayed to crew the cement trains. The limited freight on offer was simply snubbed. When I had a contract I was advised to take it home, and give them a decision in a couple of days. I could not wait. I rang them the next day to accept.

Allan was inconsolable in his grief and we had to work the full cement train shift that day. Although I was thrilled in my good fortune I actually shed tears with Allan in his pain. It was a very long shift and I was as compassionate as I could be to help him process it. I explained that there was hope he would be retained after the six months. I was so pleased when they continued his employment and changed his contract to full time permanent. Allan deserved it too. He was an excellent driver and stayed in as my trainer. I am indebted to him for putting me on a good pathway to driving. I had some logistical challenges in terms of me transferring to Burnie. The change meant an hour commute to work each day and another hour back after the shift. Two hours travel plus shift work was a challenge, but a job is a job and you had to do whatever you could to keep it. The moving of the family to Burnie would get sorted later. I was pinching myself as I was still going to be a train driver amongst the maelstrom of change.

Burnie was a busy depot. It was a major player in bulk freight. The west coast line, that runs south from Burnie, terminated there and there were log trains running west to Wiltshire Junction. The deep water port that serviced the container freight loadings meant, in my early view, that it was a place that wasn't going to shut down at least.

I had in my career witnessed a continual retraction of roles and stations, but Burnie provided security. I felt safe there. There were massive workshops, loco servicing and maintenance buildings along with sheds for basic wagon maintenance and repairs.

The Emu Bay Railway Company owned the track from Burnie to a place called Melba Flats. The E.B.R. locomotive fleet at the time consisted of the 10 and 11 class locomotives and were vacuum braked diesel hydraulics. These were only about 700hp and weighed approximately 53 tonnes. They were replaced with the larger more powerful "DQ" locomotives around the time I gained my driver's ticket and I never drove the 10 or 11 class.

The Mt Lyell mine at Queenstown carted the copper in trucks to Melba and it was loaded into rail wagons for railing to Burnie some one hundred and thirty kilometres north. A group of employees, commonly called the bulk handlers, accepted the ore trains returning from Melba. Unloading occurred by tipping the wagons upside down to empty the ore into a bin. It was then moved via a system of conveyor belts to a holding shed to await arrival of bulk ore carriers in Burnie's deep water port. The same employees loaded the boats and the ore then destined overseas.

Unloading the West Coast ore train at the tippler shed

Whilst Queenstown ore from Melba Flats was always copper, the Mine at Rosebery dug out train loadings of copper, zinc and lead. The trains arrived at Burnie with whichever commodity the mine had orders for and it was stored in very large cargo sheds on the wharf awaiting arrival of bulk ore carriers to take overseas to market, or to a refinery in Hobart.

Stabled Melba Line class 10 and 11 locomotives

What I looked forward to at Burnie was the extra contact with people and new workmates. The larger depot was going to have its characters and I was hoping to fit in.

Chapter Twenty Five: Shane Malone

Shane Malone was the supervisor at Burnie when I arrived there as a new kid on the block. Shane was apparently part of the furniture there and had spent the larger part of his career on the North West Coast. He started his career in April 1972 and finished up in October 2014.

Shane Malone

His first role was as a lad porter at Penguin. From there he moved to South Burnie as a relieving operating porter. He also had relieving positions at Somerset, Wynyard and Heybridge. He was later appointed Assistant Stationmaster at Wynyard. At twenty years of age he was believed to be the youngest ever in that role in the state.

He then was appointed to be Station Master at Ross but unfortunately the station closed down before he took up the position. He subsequently took a role as senior rail operator at Burnie under Reginald Westwood.

When the ownership of the rail network changed to A.T.N. (Australian Transport Network), Shane became the Operations Supervisor and remained in that role until retirement.

He has recalled here some of the key memories of his time on the rail.

I particularly remember the day when the general cargo freight train 244 with X class locomotives on the front arrived at Wynyard. It had travelled from Wiltshire Junction and was experiencing engine failure on the rear locomotive. The guard and fireman were standing on either side of the locomotive's footplate with the doors open. The driver, attempted to turn over the locomotive's engine in an effort to re-start them and suddenly the hapless guys were covered in oil from head to toe. It was a sight.

There was one day when the same train was slightly late arriving to Burnie and it became clear the next day as to why. In the local paper, The Advocate, *was a story that was captured by a roving reporter. A train was stopped at an area called Doctors Rocks just west of Burnie. The train was attended only by the driver with no fireman in sight. The observing reporter watched as the fireman emerged beside the locomotive and handed the driver two soft serve ice-creams. They obviously were suffering from the heat and thought it a great idea to pull up alongside the Mister Whippy ice-cream vendor positioned alongside the main highway. No-one questioned the late train.*

We used to carry a lot of livestock in specially designed livestock wagons back in the day. One day this filthy dirty great big boar arrived in an open topped "C" wagon in a crate just big enough to hold it. There were of course copious amounts of droppings in the crate and the pig was covered in it. The animal was consigned to Whiltshire but needed to be taken out of the wagon. The crate was manhandled into the baggage compartment for the journey without the guard's knowledge. The guard in the DB van was well into the section by the time his nostrils alarmed him to an almighty stink. He went through the door to the baggage compartment and was confronted by the pig and the floor covered in excrement. As the train was still only at Flowerdale and only part way to its destination the guard had no option, but to put up with the stench all the way.

Split switches

I do recall a major derailment in the Burnie yard that the author of this book was involved in. It was quite possibly the biggest yard prang I've ever witnessed Grant was driving the paper train that arrived from Boyer and consisted of approximately thirty wagons trailing into the yard. It appears the previous night shunting within the yard had resulted in the switches being split just north of the highway overpass.

Unnoticed by the ground staff they remained split and ajar of their correct setting position which always will cause a derail of a train movement coming the other way.

Grant entered the yard with his train and was winding his way down toward the shunting area when he drove into the split facing points. For some inexplicable reason other than good luck, the locomotives and about half the train of wagons had passed through the split blades of the switch without coming off the track, but one wheel flange got caught up and it resulted in every following wagon coming off the track. Grant was going slightly downslope and with plenty of horsepower proceeded to drag half his train down the yard whilst in the dirt. Upon realising the train seemed a bit harder to drive than normal he backed off the power and radioed to the rail operator on the ground that the train seems a bit sluggish. The rail operator was running along yelling, "STOP!! STOP!! For Christ's sake, STOP!!" The train stopped, but not before the resultant derailment had dragged its wagons down the yard, collected up the big loop track, the small loop track and half the right hand track of the marshalling yard. The stabled wagons on those yard tracks also got caught up in the dragnet. Hell, it was a mess. Massive cranes were brought in to separate and rerail it all.

One thing about Shane is that he has a real penchant to embellish. It *was* a big mess though.

Shane was an indoor and outdoor bowler and as we had come across each other in the sport, being friends was easy. He was pretty easy going and joined in any banter going around. If he was not initially involved he wound his way into it so as not to miss out. He revelled in the involvement of fun and I think he used it to diminish the stress and workload. It would be fair to say though, he would have been better served if he could have just kept out of it so as not to cause himself grief, but, that was Shane. He had to be in it.

*Burnie station
(courtesy of Kyle Stennings)*

As a boss, he was easy going. I probably didn't help him with the stress one day when he was down the yard writing down some wagon numbers.

He had been aware of our complaints that the photocopier and fax machine was a bit cranky. Now and then it would chew up the paper you were trying to print out. For several weeks this went on and the bloody machine kept causing grief. We were getting frustrated at the seemingly compassionless and unsympathetic replies from Shane.

When Shane was on his way back to the office my strategically positioned informant told me he was getting close, so I stuck a really large screwdriver into the machine so it looked like it was deeply embedded. I removed any covers I could and left them at angles across the machine so it looked like it was being demolished. I had a hammer and banged it on the desk. People were yelling and shouting just as Shane walked by the window. He stopped and looked in the window and for all money it looked like I was hammering the screwdriver into the machine and totally destroying it. People were pretending to hold my arms to stop me, the hammer was hitting the desk beside the machine and bits and pieces strategically placed were falling off. It was too much for Shane. His eyes widened to the size of dinner plates and he raced into the office yelling,"No, no, no!" He grabbed my arm but amid howls of laughter and people all around watching him defend his precious machine, he realised he was set up. Muttering under his breath he left the office. We had a brand new photo copier and fax within days.

On many occasions I have no doubt he thought my humour was over the top and weird, but he loved watching plans unfold and hung on every step of a prank.

What I did ponder though was the lessening of such tomfoolery at work. There were many more people but a slow shadow of properness was creeping into the workplace. To be honest it had been coming as a slow turning wheel for some time. There were shifts in behavioural standards and people were not wanting to risk offence. The willingness to take the mickey was fading and it was becoming a real risk to prank someone. I guess there are never-ending levels of a prank but without doubt the larger pre-meditated ones were becoming obsolete in the workplace.

Chapter Twenty Six: Russell Holland

Another person that I had heard about as part of the North West Coast furniture was Russell Holland. He mostly worked out of the Wynyard depot but also occasionally from Burnie. He was a person who loved a fun time at work. Russell was a dedicated railway buff and was obsessed with trains and the history of trains. He was different to me. While working I went to work, I did my job as best I could, they paid me and I went home. That was it, but Russell would eat and sleep the railway as quite a lot of employees did.

Russell with his second love
(courtesy of Helen Holland)

Russell handing the staff authority to the driver
(courtesy of Helen Holland)

Russell passed away in April 2010 at 62 years of age. His wife Helen still resides in their home in Wynyard. They occupied the railway issued house from 1968 and although not really wanting to get married at that particular time, they did so as to be eligible to have the house. Back then the supplied homes were for married employees only and the rent came out of Russell's pay. With little to their name they made it a home always. In about 1971 employees that occupied the houses were given the opportunity to purchase them. Russell and Helen scraped up the necessary deposit and over the next thirty years paid it off.

Front & rear views of Mr Ken Ferguson's first pay packet
(courtesy of Helen Holland)

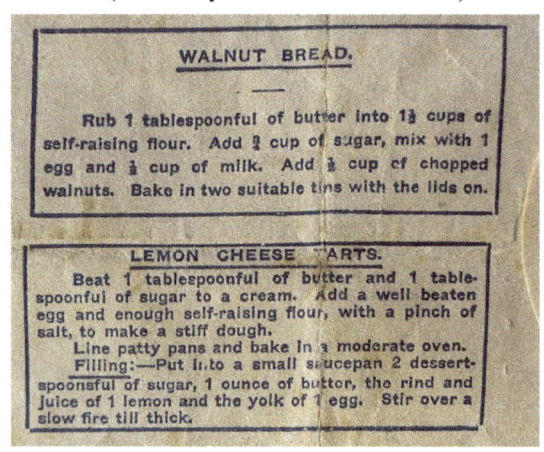

Russell was a guard for much of his career. One day he was going along in the van at the rear of the train with his stew warming nicely on the obligatory pot-belly stove. It was his favourite stew in his favourite tin dish with the metal side clips affixed to the lid to secure it on a heaving and lurching track.

The track condition west of Wynyard was very poor. Suddenly, all hell broke loose. The van bucked and lurched wildly and was derailed along with several wagons. Everything was thrown around like leaves in a tornado. The van eventually coming to rest trackside. Russell was bloodied and bruised and mightily annoyed his meal tin was squashed like a pancake among the debris. The pot belly was smashed from its fastenings and the fire coals burned Russell. The thick uniforms had offered some protection, but Russell's arms and legs suffered burns.

Crews in such circumstances were required to stay with their trains until relief or help arrived. Communications were poor and on occasions the worker's spouse knew nothing until receiving a knock on the door from the area manager the next day. When things went wrong they would be out there for sixteen or eighteen hours before getting back home.

Helen always lamented the lack of consideration afforded the families of workers back then. There was little information offered or help in a counselling sense. Families just went on with no help on how to assist a partner who was subjected to incidents, and often many serious ones, which were residual in their effects. The build up definitely had an adverse impact at home.

Russell was passionate about collecting all things railway. Since his passing, much of his collection has been gratefully accepted by the Queen Victoria Museum. Train buff's eyes would water at the items he had gathered and took pride of place in and outside his home.

Some of Russell's bits- Cap badges, ticket cutter and van key.
(courtesy of Helen Holland)

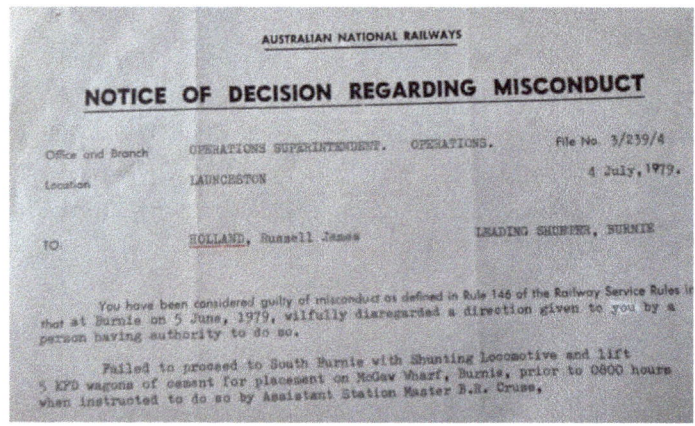

Misconduct warning earned by Russell.
(courtesy of Helen Holland)

Original ticket box repurposed
(courtesy of Helen Holland)

He, along with Helen, played a large role in the resurrection and restoration of the previously closed Mt Lyell railway. Along with a few like-minded enthusiastic volunteers they kept the rail dream alive between Queenstown and Strahan. This was subsequently taken over by the government and with commercial private operators is still running today as the world class ABT railway. Tourists from all over the world come to ride this train.

I had very little to do with Russell's territory west of Wynyard other than as a driver of the log trains down to Wiltshire Junction. With a second person or shunter on board I would drive a couple of English Electric ZB or ZC locomotives with a string of empty log wagons down and shunt them into Wiltshire log siding and return to Burnie with the previously loaded log wagons from there. The dilapidated track was scary to drive on. The bridges used to sag some inches beneath our weight and there were many dog legs in the rails. On hot summer days the bends in the rails, from expansion, defied belief that the train, even at twenty kilometres an hour, could stay on the track at all. Low speed and keeping a good lookout was essential to getting home. Diligent train handling was paramount so as not to push the track out of shape.

Disused line between Burnie and Wynyard

The untidy yard at Wiltshire was a nightmare too. The long dry grass and decrepit tracks were quite honestly embarrassing in front of the main road traffic going by.

One time the hot traction motors underneath set the long grass alight. We hurriedly reversed the locos and deft use of the fire extinguishers got us out of trouble. Luckily we noticed it early.

Diminishing freight offerings saw that line west of Burnie archived. The winding through Sister's Hills and the upkeep of culverts and bridges made it unviable.

Chapter Twenty Seven: Train driving in scenic splendour

In Burnie my driving life was great. I was working alongside the most unbelievably picturesque coastline; Burnie – Devonport is every train drivers dream! We were often hugging the seascape so closely it seemed we might fall into the briny or crash on the same rocks that the waves were hitting. Occasionally we did.

Operating trains with thundering thousands of horsepower through the many tight curves around Penguin and Goat Island was something special. As I have said, I'm not a train buff but the most benign driver would have to be at least a little bit impressed at the power and forces applied in order to get along the track there. I've always marvelled at how pulling an eight hundred metre train with thousands of horsepower through multiple tight curves at the same time doesn't pull the track out straight!

Watching the ever-changing visual landscape whilst working was a pleasure. And I got paid to do it.

New curved rail bridge in Ulverstone

Observing hundreds of sea birds in death-like dives hammering into schools of small bait fish was something special. How the hell didn't they get a headache? Maybe they do. The waves crashing over the rails laid down a salty traction benefit for us in places.

What a wonderful job in a wonderful place.

Magical seascape views between Burnie and Devonport

What better vantage point than in the cabin of a shiny new TR locomotive. In 2013 the first of 17 new TR locomotives arrived. All had entered service by May 2014. These are diesel electrics with a Caterpillar 3512 - V12 motor. Their weight is 108 tonnes and of 2000 tractive horsepower. They are equipped with a powerful dynamic brake to supplement the air brake. They cost more than $60 million and heralded the new era in locomotive upgrade of technology and capabilities. Driver interactive computer screens displaying route information and a multitude of information about the trains performance and operating requirements is a massive leap forward in safety and train operations. A replacement program of wagons included new rakes for haulage of the cement and coal traffic. New wagons to service the West Coast ore tonnage and along with new containerised freight wagons heralded the biggest modernisation and overhaul in Tasmanian rail history. The track infrastructure was massively boosted by hundreds of millions of dollars in improvements and upgrades as well. The new era of rail transport was underway in a big way and it was exciting to be a part of it.

    The West Coast track is also just as spectacular as the northern coastline, but from a different perspective. The drive begins at Burnie through suburban houses, and moves through rolling countryside and into eucalypt plantations of Surrey Hills. They seemingly go on forever.

    The ribbons of steel then move into the dry natural eucalypt forests and then southwards to the rainforests known worldwide for their beauty on Tasmania's West Coast. The high rainfall has formed an understory of moss and lichens in the sassafras and giant myrtle stands. Huge cliff faces and steep gullies are home to massive man ferns numbering in their thousands. Train wheels scream in protest as they pull through the tight curves hewn by hand from the rock. The rock faces are within touching distance from the side window of the cab while the other side shows only the very tree tops of huge trees – such is the steepness and severity of geography in these areas. Until recently chipped back a little, one cutting rock face actually hit on the side handrail of the loco as it went round the curve at thirty kilometres an hour.

    That's a tight rail track! The cuttings cut by hand are astounding testament of hard work of long ago.

Typical West Coast rock cutting
(courtesy of Barbara Hind)

All sorts of forest critters scurry from the loud vibrating intervention of their peaceful world. The Wedge-Tailed Eagles live in these parts, but hunt further north in the more open country. Occasionally one would travel the train line in search of game that the train has run over the night before. It was a smorgasbord and they just eased along at low flying height. I felt pretty special going through such visually splendid country, following an eagle flying at a height of three metres on the nose of the cab. They were never hurried. They could not exit the track until a clearing opened up trackside, but until then just quietly eased up their two metre wingspan to gently caress the air beneath in an almost slow motion display of their power and grace. On these occasions I thanked goodness for my chance to witness such a natural wonder.

Snow laden West Coast manfern

I often think about the West Coast mines and their tendency to fluctuate between vibrancy and total shutdowns. Commodity markets determine life of a mine and therefore of the towns reliant on them. They flutter like butterflies on a market breeze. I certainly hope they continue so that other train drivers can indulge in this wonderful place.

  A mining accident closed down the Queenstown mine in 2013; Melba Flats closed and trains now only travel from Burnie to Rosebery and back.

  That part of the track had a couple of interesting parts. There is a tunnel that runs through a hill just prior to bursting out and into the Melba yard. It is four hundred metres in length and was built for the much smaller locomotives, but we travelled through it with our larger DQ class. The tunnel track bed was lowered. The thirty centimetre communications aerials on the cabs folded over as the train progressed through the tunnel.

The Melba Tunnel. (courtesy of Kyle Stennings)

Another place of note is the "croc pit". This place was named so because of its appearance. It was essentially a brackish dark body of water that was trapped on the top side of the railway embankment. It was in a deep dark gully surrounded by a tall canopy of forest trees. Next to no sunlight gets in and it looks a foreboding place. The water is still and stagnant and there is no flowing water passing through. Rotten fallen logs float, but are never moved around as no breeze gets in either. It resembles a scene from the hinterland of the Daintree. The floating logs look like real crocodiles. It is an eerie area. The track on either side of the gully descends on approach to the croc pit. Once adjacent to the croc pit it is then very steep to get up and out. We often struggled because of the steepness and load, but the big killer was the damp atmosphere. The sap falling onto the rail from the tree canopy did not help. This, coupled with rust on the steel rail from only intermittent usage, meant a very greasy connection causing tractive effort from the locomotives to be reduced. With the wheel slip light illuminated and the amp gauge shouting protest we would use all our experience to try to get up the bank. Sandboxes pouring sand onto the track often helped us out.

On one occasion I had to reverse the train back down the hill and back up the other side a little in order to get enough speed and momentum to have a chance to get up again. It was times like this we largely disregarded the designated track speed for the section. Judgement of speed, momentum and deft power application was critical in order to get out of the croc pit. Luck sometimes was helpful.

The "croc pit". (courtesy of Kyle Stennings)

Once over the bank we could thunder along with all four locomotives singing a melody that shook the leaves and ground all around. The valuable copper cargo would get to its destination.

Moory Junction in mid-winter, Melba Line

Snow covered track near Guildford, Melba Line

Two prominent uphill grades on the way were the Boco bank and Hatfield bank. Both were over many kilometres in length and even at full power we would only reach around twenty six kilometres an hour. This was 'flat stick' and would shake the plant and animal kingdoms all around us as we went up them.

The DQ locomotives are my favourites. They are reliable and on the challenging geography of the West Coast, they will dig down deep when the going got tough. At 91.5 tonnes and 1500hp and it matters not a wet and greasy rail or a chock-full load tonnage, they never give up or argued the toss. A different driver skillset was required on this track and its conditions. The overhead tree canopy sometimes met each other above and created a cave like path through the cuttings. This allowed for a lot of sap and debris from the trees to land on the railhead and coupled with drizzle and a rusty film, it caused slippage and had potential to actually stop the train or at least slow to single figure speeds. The DQ'S were like any other loco, quick to drop away from high speed under these conditions, but would grind away all day at lower speed and get you home. The knotched throttle was a bonus for secure incremental asking of power. If you allowed the locomotives to talk to you and if you listened to them and their needs they would reward you. Coaxing and massaging your train with good train management skills is the answer on this track.

The concrete and steel girder Bastyn Bridge is another awesome sight. It carries the train over the Pieman River with the Bastyn Dam built to hold back the waters of Lake Rosebery standing resolute some one hundred metres upstream. The bridge is about one hundred metres above the river and when the dam is overflowing the spray and fine mist is stunning. It drifts onto the locomotive windows as we drive over the bridge. When the dam's hydro turbines are running the river turns into a washing machine beneath us. It's very spectacular.

I did wonder some things as I travelled over the bridge. Things like how often these steel structures are inspected for metal fatigue. Also what might happen if the dam bursts?

There clearly is not the capacity to easily stop the train if things are not good.

Special passenger train on the Bastyn Bridge
(courtesy of Helen Holland)

One thing I do know for sure is that when coming downhill with a train of fifteen hundred tonnes, a bridge intact and where it should be is very important. It's fair to say that I have a massive appreciation for the engineering of bridges.

I had only the one derailment in all my years on the mainline. Yard derailments however were numerous. There was so much human action involved in yard shunting and therefore more scope for human error. Mostly these were minor, with a bogie set off or a wagon off here and there. Maybe a miscalculation of judgement would mean the push movement of a wagon to go over the dead end or derail blocks.

Buffer stop setup at track dead end

Split switches are probably the most common cause of all derailments in a yard. This means that one wheel of the leading bogie being asked to go up one track and the other wheel asked to go up another. Split switches never end well.

Chapter Twenty Eight: The joy of it all

One particularly joyful aspect is to witness the glee and excitement of pedestrians and those living trackside at the sight of an approaching train. I am not sure where the attraction starts, but there is and has always been a fascination around trains. It is possibly in part derived from the early American films depicting the wild west and the early settlers opening up the land. The hardship that they endured was eased by the arrival of train lines and big steel monsters belching steam and power; a respectful understanding of their worth from very early days.

Or maybe it's the mystic aura of steam and ash from locomotives powering up a bank. The power and noise of a train in full voice seems to result in an excitement rush in millions of people around the world and it matters not the type of locomotive or train.

Train spotters and enthusiasts travel all over the globe and get to know and experience the different rail systems and the country or scenery they travel through. Some are besotted by them. The trains have this magnetic appeal and some don't even know why.

Trains heading through the Pyrenees mountains of Europe; the Orient Express; Underground trains in large cities; or the North to South outback Ghan train in Australia; all have a magnetic attraction.

I also think its the excitement of adventure that stirs in all of us as we wait at the station. We know what happens. A train pulls up and we get on and the train whisks us away, but no matter how many times it happens there is always still the same anticipation next time.

This passion of people was evident as I travelled along the North West Coast. People of all ages raced out to their backyards and particularly children climbed atop the paling fences oblivious to their skin being grazed. People trackside jostled for the best vantage points and even those uninterested still gave their attention even if only momentarily. Parents and children all waved and the expectation and gaining of a whistle pop was heightened as I waved to all. A whistle pop created faces of appreciation among the crowd. Grazed skin was only attended to when the last carriage was gone from the sight of longing eyes.

I was once one of those children, hoping to one day drive that train.

For my last ten years as a driver I dressed in a Santa Claus suit and hat for the entire month of December whenever I drove a train. The children that spotted me got to know my shifts and would have the entire family trackside on the next shift. It generated a groundswell of goodwill and the local newspaper ran a story on it.

Train driving Santa

Later years saw Tasrail running a number of their locomotives with Christmas lights which was a spectacular hit with the community. Darkness saw throngs of people following the trains to view a moving Christmas scene. It was special.

Locomotives decorated with Christmas lights

In the last ten years of my career I became a driver trainer. My primary role was still driving the trains, but I had a trainee on board to learn the things it takes to make a train driver.

On some occasions I also had a fully qualified driver from interstate or even overseas who wanted a change. The industry often searched for these people to compliment the roster numbers. However, the fully qualified drivers still need to learn our locomotive fleet and the track geography. Despite coming from the Pilbara or the northern New South Wales coal regions, many were still brought undone by our geography and tight narrow track. The iron ore trains in the Pilbara for example are transport routes of massive proportions that by Tasmanian standards are difficult to comprehend. They have huge four thousand horse power locomotives hauling three kilometre long strings of wagons numbering in their hundreds.

Pilbara ore train
(courtesy of Kyle Stennings)

The Queensland and New South Wales coal regions and the wheat belt areas of mainland Australia also boast large scale rail operations. Many drivers coming from these other places attest to the difficulty of our West Coast terrain with some of them not coping and leaving. Sometimes they think of it as a tree change while others just need to experience a difference. All agree at the quieter pace and more leisurely feel of our rail.

These incoming drivers had to learn to adapt and were mostly good to go. The depot at Burnie, with a few exceptions, was all the better for their coming.

The trainees were a different matter. They were usually drafted from the rail operators and as such had already grown somewhat in the business. Their transition was much more fluent than if taken cold off the street. Tasrail began a trainee induction program that had gathered dust for decades. Forecast freight volume increases and improved customer satisfaction and faith in freight movement meant driver ranks needed a bolster.

Burnie trainees were assigned to me. It had been my desire to impart my knowledge and skillsets for a long time and I was determined to fulfil the role to the best of my ability. With my guidance they would learn to drive trains just as Allan had helped me many years earlier. I was hoping to do him proud. Like me, the trainees could not believe their good fortune to be given the opportunity.

As I drove along and explained what I was doing and why, the trainees would soak up the sights and sounds around them. I often talked in advance of the train's movement so they could witness it unfold like a moving screen and therefore could see and feel the results of my actions. This was far better than obtaining information in a retrospective fashion. I loved to show off, but in a respectful way. They needed to know I could do it well so as to nurture respect and a want to achieve a high level. I never ever expected them to drive like me or try to. Every single driver is an individual and their driving will also be individual to them. My task was to teach them to drive to standards accepted and expected by the rail company.

I reckon I had an easy style of teaching. I had pride well up in me as I watched them "get it". All trainees on their first trip with me were subjected to a talk fest. Getting to know each other was very important. I made it clear that whatever the question, it was not a silly one.

On the second trip before we drove off I would ask them to sit for a moment in the driver's seat and imagine themselves operating the train. I would ask, "Would you still like to be a train driver?" The reply was always yes. Then I would say, "Well then drive!" It was always met with an unbelievable astonishment, but not one trainee said no. I told them that I would stand beside them at their shoulder for as long as it takes for them to feel comfortable. I did so until they said; "It's ok, I've got this".

Clearly, for any tricky bits and scary track areas I would take over, but in the other parts it was special to watch their confidence grow. My sense of pride in them was immeasurable and I would have done it for free.

They began their journey.

Chapter Twenty Nine: Kyle Stennings

My first trainee was Kyle Stennings and he has recounted some of his career below.

Kyle Stennings in his happy place

I started as a track fettler in March 2010. On my second day on the job I was travelling as a passenger with others in a gang truck. We were driving to Penguin and following behind us was a motorised sleeper inserter vehicle being driven by another of our gang members. The vehicle had somehow managed to become stuck on the road level crossing whilst traversing it. Our truck driver declared that he would free him up. With that our driver proceeded to throw our truck into reverse and piled into the sleeper vehicle. The shaken driver poked his head out of the canvas awning and began gesturing fiercely at us in the truck.

Retired sleeper inserter

The same day a track jack vehicle was driving down to the other end of the Penguin level crossing and forgot to lift the hydraulic clamp feet. It hit the bitumen and propelled the driver clean out of the vehicle. I thought to myself, I've landed a very interesting job here at the railway. It was straight out of the comedy F Troop.

Welding track gang in operation
(courtesy of Kyle Stennings)

After six months I moved over to the thermit welding gang. We replaced the bolted joints with welded rail joints.

In 2011 I became a rail operator in Burnie working under supervisor Shane Malone. Rail Operator was the new term for shunter. I performed this role in Burnie for approximately two years. Marshalling wagons to and from Burnie's Toll wharf was challenging. We often had waves crashing over us after they collided onto the rocks and the concrete break wall. On occasions when high tides and howling winds from the often belligerent Bass Strait came roaring in from the north, the cascading waves completely engulfed our locomotives and wagons.

Wharf and sea at Burnie
(courtesy of Kyle Stennings)

Walking up and down the yard out there meant being vigilant at all times. It was a hub of activity and forklifts were buzzing about like huge noisy bumblebees on steroids. Road trucks were lining up for service a dozen at a time. It seemed it was roughly organised chaos. We often sheltered from the drenching waves by hugging closely to the wagons, but we also did it because it just felt safer.

I was appointed to the position of trainee driver with Driver Trainer Grant Youd as my teacher, in June 2013. We had a ball. Great fun and laughs aplenty. Don't get me wrong, we did our job, but we made sure that it was enjoyable. I felt at home on the locomotive as if it was where I needed to be.

My teacher often pulled rank on me and I would be subjected to listening to hours of opera music on the cd player in the cab. He said I needed some culture and an expansion of taste. I actually think he was more a fan of studying people's grimaces than of opera. When the ground rail operators in the yard hopped up into the cab to talk to us they often just turned around and went back out again rather than give him the satisfaction of victory in the war against their senses.

One particular funny thing was when we set up the illusion that we were both studying the bible while going down the track. We each took to work a copy and left them in our bags, but with a portion of the good book sticking out for any enquiring eye to feast upon. It was so funny to watch someone walk by our bags with a sideways glance. Sometimes they would stop and double check. We continued this for months and even to the most sceptical of our workmates it was becoming more and more real. We would occasionally speak quotes from its text to cement the prank. We only knew two or three. Obviously we had to find some balance between the ridiculous and the believable. Whenever we were challenged we would quote our couple of known bits and had markers in the bibles to validate and show them. It was a very apparent conversion to the ways of the Lord. Amen.

Our bible studies prank

I resigned from Tasrail to go drive iron ore trains in the Pilbara in the Western Australia in March 2017. The difference in scale is incredible in every sense of the word. It was the pinnacle in train driving for me.

The difference in scale can however be replicated as well when things go horribly wrong. On the 5th of November 2018, a train of approximately three kilometres in length was derailed and compressed in length to about three hundred metres, such was the massive forces involved. The company just sent in a group of massive bulldozers and shoved the mess aside and replaced the tracks to get the revenue side of things back under control. They took ten days to get it running again and sorted out the mess of wagons, rails, and ore later.

Pilbara crash
(courtesy of Kyle Stennings)

When the trains arrive at Port Hedland they are set up by the train drivers who then get off. The trains are then unloaded by being tipped upside down, multiple wagons at a time, into a six story deep bin. The amazing thing is that the unloading is done by a guy sitting in an office in Perth. Remote controlled unloading from thousands of kilometres away. How amazing is that!

Port Hedland has four or five ore carrier boats moving in and out at any given time. It's a very busy port with tugs operating twenty four hours a day.

Another challenge in western Australia is the weather. A place called Jimble Bar can make fifty degrees in summer and get down to minus ten in winter.

I also recall being stuck up there in my temporary billeting quarters ('Donga') and sitting out Cyclone Veronica. The cyclone was one hundred and five kilometres wide. To give perspective, Cyclone Tracy could fit inside the eye of Cyclone Veronica. Obviously, the red alert had us all bunkered down for our safety and the four to five hundred millimetres of rain over two days was a huge total. We were down for a week with no work. It's fair to say the weather up there knows very few boundaries.

Cyclone Veronica
(courtesy of Kyle Stennings)

After two and a half years I returned to Tasmanian rail and re-joined the Burnie depot. It was small in scale, but varied in its own way.

Once I was stuck overnight in the Rosebery yard with the train because of a big snowfall. I was put up for the night and supplied a comfy bed, meals and a few drinks for my bother. The road was also blocked due to the snow, but the train was stabled largely because of the number of downed trees. The trees succumb to the sheer weight of snow and coupled with damp soft soil they tumble down over the track. The track guys came out the next morning to clear them away and allow the train through.

One time that was a bit scary was when travelling south just near the Natone Road crossing. There was a downed set of powerlines and they were hanging at about cab height. I threw the train into "emergency" and hit the floor. The powerlines danced all about the windows and door of the locomotive. I contacted the relevant people and stayed put in the locomotive until the power company came and fixed things up.

In November 2021, I cemented my role as a rail foamer (a term for train buff) when I fulfilled a lifelong dream by privately purchasing a fully operational working two thousand, five hundred and fifty horsepower, ZA class English Electric locomotive from Tasrail. It was surplus to their needs, but I was elated to have it soon take up residence at my beloved Don River Railway yards in Devonport.

Kyle Stennings.

Kyle's privately owned English Electric locomotive
(courtesy of Kyle Stennings)

Kyle still drives for Tasrail and will be for a long time yet. I have passed the baton to many trainees such as Kyle. They will also encounter much change throughout their careers.

I retired from Tasrail on 30th July 2021.

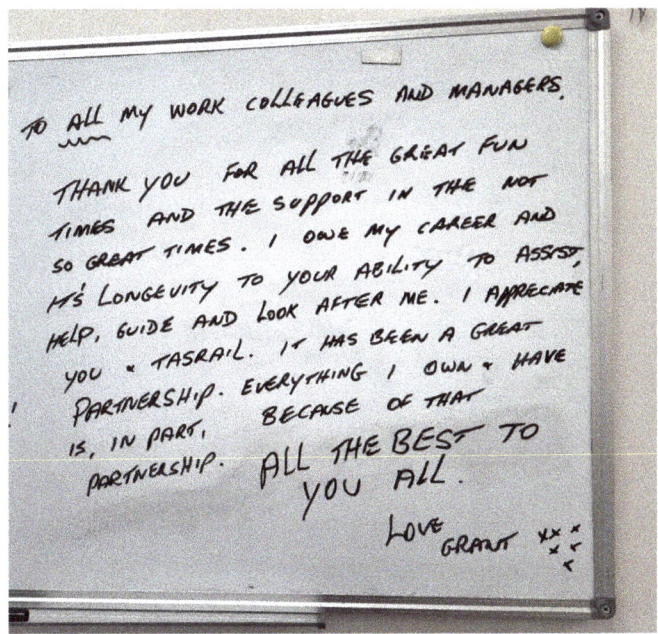

Final day message

Chapter Thirty: Looking back

Over the last couple of decades it has become apparent that with the transition from a community-based rail system to a business-focussed freight transport system, some loss of fun has occurred. It was inevitable here as is the case everywhere else. Every workplace nowadays needs to strive for and maintain continuous improvement of standards in health and safety and workplace behaviour is fiercely sought. The procedures, policies and regulatory controls are enforcing the way work is done. It is vastly different from my early years.

The modern world demands political correctness, gender equality, inclusivity, alcohol and drug policies, unfair dismissal laws and improved behavioural standards. The list is endless. Mind you, from the employer viewpoint, it is necessary and litigation protection is nowadays gold. The managing of people throughout the business has become a skill set of managers and as necessary as water. As nostalgic as it is to look back on the pranks and fun of the early days and yearn for their return, the truth is that change is inevitable. Small changes or big, it matters not. We are evolving as each second ticks by so I guess it's nothing new.

If I were to ask anything it is for each of us to look back occasionally so you can see where you have come from. If you do not, then how do you know how far you have come? In this book, I have looked back and it's only then that I realised the journey that I've been on.

I could not write a book about my life on the railway without discussing collisions with road vehicles. It brings much distress to all train drivers and rail system managers.

The pain and suffering goes far beyond that felt at the physical crash site. An accident at a level crossing is like throwing a pebble into a pond. The ripples travel outward and their touch is felt by many. Unlike the ripples in the pond that diminish to nothing eventually, trauma felt due to such confronting incidents travel on forever and never arrive at a shore.

Tasrail spends much time and effort on safety awareness and continually upgrades its infrastructure. It engages at all levels in an effort to work towards zero harm.

I have lost count of the number of near misses and actual incidents that have dotted my career and the effect on me and my family, has been profound. Pulling people, particularly children, out of mangled cars is not pleasant. They are damaged physically and mentally. Even though as a driver I had done all I could to avoid it.

The senselessness of it all.

I lament the fact that humans are fraught with judgement errors. We and machines often do not get it right, but we must find a way, because the cost is too great.

For many years I've been thankful to Tasrail in allowing me to be a part of the effort to bring about change. In my own time and with support from Tasrail, I have spoken at a number of public forums and community groups in an effort to promote awareness around our level crossings. I attended schools and addressed groups of a hundred students who were about to obtain their car licences. Almost always these talks would result in tears creeping down my face. On one occasion, a television crew interviewed me in my own loungeroom and the emotion and distress was clear for all to see on national television. This was confronting, but the message was clear; obey the laws and stay safe. The rail level crossing is a shared space.

Although my career is at its end, I pray that we all stay safe around trains.

www.ingramcontent.com/pod-product-compliance
Lightning Source LLC
Chambersburg PA
CBHW040741020526
44107CB00084B/2835